Business Development Culture

Business Development Culture

Taking sales culture beyond the sales team

Alex Moyle

KoganPage

First published in Great Britain and the United States in 2018 by Kogan Page Limited

2nd Floor, 45 Gee Street	c/o Martin P Hill Consulting	4737/23 Ansari Road
London	122 W 27th St, 10th Floor	Daryaganj
EC1V 3RS	New York NY 10001	New Delhi 110002
United Kingdom	USA	India

www.koganpage.com

ISBN   978 0 7494 8191 9
E-ISBN   978 0 7494 8192 6

British Library Cataloguing-in-Publication Data

A CIP record for this book is available from the British Library.

Library of Congress Cataloging-in-Publication Data
Names: Moyle, Alex, author.
Title: Business development culture : taking sales culture beyond the sales
    team / Alex Moyle.
Description: New York, NY : Kogan Page Ltd, [2018] | Includes index.
Identifiers: LCCN 2018030635 (print) | LCCN 2018031490 (ebook) | ISBN
    9780749481926 (ebook) | ISBN 9780749481919 (pbk.)
Subjects: LCSH: Organizational change. | Strategic planning. | Teams in the
    workplace. | Selling.
Classification: LCC HD58.8 (ebook) | LCC HD58.8 .M69 2018 (print) | DDC
    658.8/1–dc23

Typeset by Integra Software Services, Pondicherry
Print production managed by Jellyfish
Printed and bound by 4edge Limited, UK

This book would not have been finished without the unending support of my amazing wife.
Lisa, I love you.

To my sons, work hard, live your dreams.

CONTENTS

ACKNOWLEDGEMENTS

During the writing of this book, I received advice and support from many people. Without the support of the individuals below the book would not be what it is today:

John Argent – CEO, Six
James Vowles – CCO, Tangle Teezer
Phil Jones MBE – MD, Brother UK
Declan Sharpe – Senior VP Sales, Iomart
Peter Belsey
Ben Turner – APS
Nick Lee – Professor, Warwick Business School
Nicky Lloyd – Six
Charlotte Owen – Kogan Page
Theodore Mason – CEO, Simitive
Roisin Woolnough
Banking Standards Board
Nicky Lloyd – Six

Introduction to business development culture

Thank you for taking the time to pick up this book. It has been a long time in the making but I've enjoyed writing it. Mostly!

I have been involved in sales in one shape or form for a long time. You could say my sales career started when I used to bulk buy cans of coke to sell on the bus during school trips or when I used to travel to the United States in my university holidays to sell educational books door to door. The reality, though, is that my career as a sales professional started properly 20 years ago when I became a professional recruiter. I know for many readers the words 'professional' and 'recruiter' do not normally sit in the same sentence. However, back then, recruitment was a local and relationship-driven market, which meant I had to be a sales professional as well as a recruiter. What about today's market? I would argue that being local and relationship-driven is more important than ever. Why? Because it's all about what the customer needs and wants.

Before we go any further, we need to talk about the word 'sales'. I cannot remember a time when the phrase 'I'm in sales' has been met with anything other than apprehension or suspicion. It sits in a bucket alongside other professions such as an estate agent, a recruiter or a financial advisor. All of these professionals are viewed with scepticism and caution – at best. The word 'sales' and the act of 'selling' are toxic, the inference being that to 'sell', you need to be pushy and force something on someone that they do not need or want, where in reality the opposite is true. The irony is that an organization's willingness and ability to 'sell' has never been more important but still the negative sales reputation sticks.

That's largely why I felt compelled to write this book. Organizations need to foster a sales-focused business development culture and not just in the sales team: it needs to exist throughout the whole business, from senior management to the most junior roles, from finance to IT. Some organizations have embraced this idea and are enjoying healthy, stable growth and profits as a result of their sales-focused business development culture. Other organizations have a long way to go. Let's look at why this journey is so important and why now, today.

Why is selling so important today?

Speak to ex-bookshop owners, ex-Yellow Pages sales reps, ex-travel agents or newspaper publishers and you will soon realize the impact the 'digital revolution' has had on their industry and their livelihoods. It has totally disrupted the business models in these sectors. Other sectors have not been impacted in the same way. Not yet. Professional services, for example, has been relatively insulated from the impact of the digital revolution up until now. But that is changing and it's changing fast.

'As a CEO you have to recognize that your business will be radically different in the next 5 to 10 years and then build and lead a team to succeed in that new world.' So said Adena Friedman,[1] CEO of the financial services company, Nasdaq Inc, in KPMG's 2017 Global CEO Outlook report. Called *Disrupt and Grow*, the professional services company's report found that CEOs are all too aware of the possibility that wholesale change is on the horizon; 74 per cent of the CEOs taking part in the survey said their organization was striving to be the disruptor in their sector, knowing that if they aren't they will be the disrupted.

If your industry has not been disrupted by the digital revolution yet, then prepare for it. It will happen and you need to be ready for it. Don't believe me? There are many corporate case studies that sound as a warning bell for organizations that do not adapt to change. There's Kodak, the firm that invented digital photography, but refused to adapt their business model and eventually went POP. There's the Blockbuster video franchise. Many of you readers will remember spending hours wandering around Blockbuster stores arguing with friends and partners about what video to watch. Along came streaming and... POP. There's Yell.com, the business advertising and listing business. They woke up one day and someone else was doing what they did for free... POP. Your Yellow Pages is now only 15 per cent of what it used to be.

Businesses are being hit by a series of challenges; an almost unlimited supply of free knowledge, automation of previously technically challenging tasks (stock trades, tax returns, bookkeeping, applicant sourcing, buying insurance, etc), and most worryingly for service firms, by the fact that buyers are increasingly willing to sacrifice some 'feeling' of quality for a reduced price (fixed price recruiters, virtual accountants, centralized conveyancing and the like).

Customers are increasingly able to perform activities that would previously have been outsourced, such as recruiting, accounting and marketing. There's also the issue of lower priced competition. Pricing is much more transparent than ever before, giving customers a greater awareness of the pricing structures between you and your competitors. Plus, there is increased usage of procurement or outsourced providers to manage the cost of the supplier base; we now have preferred supplier lists.

For many established professional service companies wanting to succeed, it is no longer enough to say 'We are good at what we do' or 'We have always delivered on time.' It is not enough for any business because the market is too competitive and there are too many new entrants looking to innovate, automate or commoditize to succeed. Sometimes the process of commoditization means a race to the bottom where quality is always sacrificed for price.

The commoditization of the service sector is causing so much disruption now because its business models have traditionally been sheltered from normal market forces. Loyalty has typically been high because these companies 'understand our business' and it would be too much work to change. They didn't need to go for the hard sell. New clients were acquired because you knew them from another firm or you met them a few years ago at a conference. High fees were tolerated because your knowledge and your skills in applying them were seen as a mystic dark art. That's all changing now.

The combination of easy access to knowledge, technological automation, globalization, open pricing and a willingness of the buyer to sacrifice some quality for a lower price means that professional service firms are, for the first time, facing the same commercial pressures as other industries, such as retail, leisure, travel and telecom. These industries have, for many years, had to exist in an environment of low customer loyalty, price visibility between competitors and having to provide more for less. They have built their business models on the basis that they need to devote a significant amount of time and effort every day to continuously win, retain and expand their existing customer base.

That is what professional services are going to have to do. The challenge many of them face is that 'business development' and 'sales' activities are often seen as unseemly. Ideally, it is left to the sales team or the partners or directors of the firm. The traditional approach is that if sales activities must be performed, then it happens when you first start out and are building up your book of business or when the fee pipeline is low. The consequence of this type of approach is that either firms get stuck in a cycle of feast and famine, or far worse, they become trapped having to work for clients that are unprofitable because some revenue is better than none in the absence of a pipeline of new and more profitable clients.

From my research I see very few in professional services who deny the need to change. According to *The Future of General Insurance 2016*, research by the customer experience management company, Market Force, 77 per cent of insurance organizations think the industry's appetite for innovation had increased in the previous 12 months. Moreover, 73 per cent were waiting for the 'Uber moment' to arrive and totally disrupt the market. Everyone knows that change is inevitable.[2]

However, customer loyalty programmes or launching new products do not replace the need of almost every professional service business to find more customers that want their service and are willing to pay for it. And therein lies the rub.

You are probably thinking 'So what? Where is the news here Alex?' The news is that my most startling finding when I talk to professional services firms is their reluctance to adopt a proactive approach to finding new clients and retaining and expanding existing clients. Phrases I hear regularly include 'I do not want to tell my client about our other services or they might think I am being pushy' and 'I don't do cold calls, I only call people I know' and 'That's my client – I do not want anyone to call them.'

In today's market, where professional service firms need more new customers than ever before, organizations simply cannot afford to let these kinds of cultural beliefs continue. This book will help you change those mindsets.

Who this book is for

This book can help all sales professionals, but in particular it will help all companies who sell services business to business. Yet the term 'services' is a broad one, so let me explain a little more about who within the business to business services community will enjoy this book.

Group 1: People who have never previously had to sell

Across the whole business to business services community there are individuals who are now expected to sell where they have never had to before. In law firms, accounting firms, and many other professional service companies – like engineering consultancies – the need to sell is moving down from the partner/director group to all levels of the organization, for example the audit senior who is now expected to look for potential upsell opportunities while on audit. These individuals never signed up to be in a sales role, but yet are now involved in the process.

Group 2: People who sell a service and deliver the service they have sold

This group does not consist of full-time salespeople but they sell their services and then are responsible for the delivery of the services they sell. They range from financial advisors to partners of legal or accounting firms, recruiters, training companies, directors in marketing agencies and many others.

More competition, commoditization and more convoluted sales processes (ie multiple stakeholders) mean this group needs to spend more time selling as their traditional clients are switching to technology-driven solutions, bringing services in-house or are now participating in formal pitch processes, whereas previously these people enjoyed trusted advisor status.

Group 3: Sales professionals that have switched from selling products to solutions

As traditional business models are disrupted, more firms are switching their focus from selling products to service solutions. This would include printing companies who now offer outsourced print solutions, IT services companies who used to sell servers and now offer cloud-based solutions. The challenge for this group of already sales professionals is that selling services requires a more consultative approach, with longer sales cycles and a multiple stakeholder sales process, which, in many instances, represents a big shift in approach.

A bit about how this book works...

Before we go any further, I want you to know what you will get from reading this book. It would be unrealistic for me to say that I will provide answers to every challenge that I highlight. Who could do that? I will also not provide you with any guarantees of foolproof solutions to these challenges. Quite simply, when you are working to change the behaviour of individuals it is pretty much impossible to say with absolute certainty what will happen in any given situation. In short, I am not a prophet delivering salvation to your business development challenges.

The good news is that, in all the time I have spent with CEOs, partners and sales directors, I have never met one that was in search of a prophet. Phew. This is mainly because these individuals were already clear on the journey they wanted to travel. What they weren't clear on was how to get from where they were to where they wanted to be tomorrow. That is a conundrum that many leaders face.

This book is intended to be a collection of techniques, strategies and approaches that you can use in your own organization.

I hope that after your first read, you keep coming back to the book as a source of reference when you are looking for techniques and exercises to better engage your teams. Importantly, the insights and exercises are not just my own – they are gathered from numerous CEOs such as Phil Jones, CEO of Brother UK. I have also drawn on the insights and exercises from other subject matter experts and, of course, I offer you my own experiences and insights, gained from over 20 years in the industry.

I have encountered some challenges when writing the book and I feel it is only fair to share them with you. The most significant challenge has been finding a balance between covering the full breadth of 'cultural change', while at the same time providing enough depth on each topic to provide useful and relevant insights. The central premise of this book is that business development culture belongs to the whole organization rather than just the sales team. This means that over the course of the book, I cover a wide variety of topics, but I can't always go into those topics in as much detail as I would like, otherwise this book would have been a lot larger than it is now!

As with all books, you will take the most from chapters where you have the most need, so certain topics are bound to grab your attention more than others.

References

1 Friedman, A (2017) *Disrupt and Grow*, KPMG global CEO outlook report
2 Marketforce.eu.com (2016) *The Future of General Insurance 2016* http://events.marketforce.eu.com/GIReport2016 [last accessed 14/4/18]

PART ONE
Adapting to change is the new normal

Like it or not, change is happening or will happen across every industry sector. Some markets have already witnessed wholesale disruption, courtesy of the digital revolution. Some are at the early stages of disruption and a few are still relatively unscathed. What is for sure is that change is happening or going to happen for every business in every sector and it will keep happening. The impact of globalization, technology, lower barriers to entry and changes to how people buy services is challenging every firm's business model. This means that businesses now need to do business differently. And in two years' time, the rules may have all changed again. Change is the new constant, which presents certain challenges for organizations.

The question for every company is this: **How do we adapt what we do to thrive in a fast-changing world, rather than survive or, at worst, simply disappear?**

This is not a new question for business leaders to ask. However, what is new is the pace of change and the fact that it is now constant.

This speed of change causes two challenges in particular. Firstly, there are market-based challenges. These challenges are typically driven by customer demands, such as what they want to buy and the way they want to buy it (wanting to conduct personal banking without visiting a branch, being able to order a cab at 11.30pm without having to call around a number of firms...). New or existing competitors will often redesign services to meet customer demand, which then gives them a competitive advantage (an example of this is the creation of online share trading platforms to create a lower cost delivery model over traditional stockbrokers). The economic environment will influence not only what people are willing to buy but also their ability to pay the 'traditional' price paid – their 'real' demand.

The second area of challenge is around the core culture of an organization. Core culture-based challenges are the issues associated with how an organization's people, processes and leadership are able to adapt the way they operate to meet customer demand. The heart of the challenge for most leaders is overcoming the 'friction' of moving from their current culture ('we have always done it this way'), to a culture that is ready to meet customer demands.

There are so many preconceived notions about what sales involves and how it makes people feel, that changing it involves a cultural shift away from the initiative-led approach that companies traditionally take.

This section of the book focuses on understanding the market and cultural challenges companies are facing.

The challenges of a changing market

Industries such as retail and manufacturing have had to be agile and adaptable in order to survive the erosion of margins from automation, globalization and other forces for decades now. Other sectors have had it easier, but those days are over. The drivers of commoditization, globalization, automation, reintermediation (Uber enabling users to get a taxi from wherever they are) and disintermediation (companies selling direct from websites) are now omnipresent. Even professional services firms, relatively insulated from these forces of change up until recently, are now feeling the pinch.

So why has it taken so long for professional services to face disruption on the scale of other sectors? Because the intrinsic 'value' of a service is built on four pillars of value and disruption of those pillars has been slow. But now that the disruption has started, the speed of change has escalated rapidly.

Before we go any further, let's establish what the four pillars of value are:

1 **Knowledge**: I know how to do things you do not.

2 **Application**: I know how to apply my knowledge to your specific situation.

3 **Peace of mind**: My service gives you the reassurance you need that the right thing has been done at the right time.

4 **Inertia against change**: My clients know me and trust me so they will not leave me.

But these pillars have now been shaken for a number of reasons.

Value of knowledge

The Internet has democratized knowledge and how we buy products and services. Can you remember the last time you went into a travel agent to pick up brochures and book a holiday? No, neither can I. If I did go to a travel agent, I would already know more about where I want to go and the hotels I am interested in than the travel agent I am speaking to. I would have done my research via the Internet before my visit.

It is this accessibility of knowledge that is changing how people and organizations buy services. It has also demystified what a lot of industries offer. Historically, many roles within the B2B services sector (ie professional services) have been shrouded in mystery. For example, the stockbroker: 'Let me tell you which shares to buy.' Or the recruiter: 'I have a network of people I know.' Or the lawyer: 'Let me tell you what the law says.' Or the marketer: 'I can generate you leads.'

The Internet provides much of this information and, what's more, it's free. I no longer need to pay my accountant to find out if an expense is allowable as I can look it up myself. I no longer need to ask a stockbroker for share tips when I can do my own research. And I no longer need to use a recruiter when I have a network of my own that I can leverage. And it's not just me that can do all this. Look back a few years when CFOs had to pay their accountants to come in and explain the impact of new accounting standards. Fast forward to the present day and now the same accounting firm has probably produced a free white paper and 'how to guide'. Accountancy firms are now giving their knowledge away for free because that's what the market demands.

While some of us might think knowledge still has value, in terms of this first pillar, the ubiquitous stream of content marketing material (how to guides, tip sheets, white papers, social media platforms...) demonstrates that professional service companies are increasingly willing to share their knowledge for free.

Try it out

Exercise: Pick a leadership, sales, marketing or training challenge you currently have. Type into any search engine 'How do I solve <insert challenge>' and see what response you get. You'd be surprised by how much you get for free.

Exercise: Pick a problem that you typically solve for your customers. Type into any search engine 'How do I solve <insert problem>' and see how much your customers can get for free. Then look to see how many of your competitors are giving away knowledge.

This increased access to knowledge has had a huge impact on the way that we now buy goods and services. Our purchasing habits are now based around what Google calls the Zero Moment of Truth (ZMOT or ZeeMOT). Google's premise is that in the days before the Internet, when we had a need for a product or a service, we would visit a few shops. This was the first moment of truth. Our second moment of truth came when we assessed the 'experience' after we had bought the product or service. In today's marketplace, Google's research shows that before we even interact with an organization we have probably 'googled' them and researched them. And this behaviour isn't that new: back in 2011 Google found that '79 per cent of shoppers used mobile to help with shopping', as evidenced in the 2011 ebook *ZMOT: Winning the Zero Moment of Truth*.[1]

What this shows is that there has been a fundamental change in how we buy products and services. It has taken many professional services leaders a long time to realize that this also applies to their customers. Some leaders haven't even realized it yet. Despite the fact that many professional services leaders are digitally savvy in how they research and buy things, they have not realized that their customers are doing the same about their service.

Think for a moment about how you would approach buying some sales training for your team. You would probably do the following:

- Email friends or colleagues and ask for recommendations.
- Type into Google 'Sales training for <insert job function>'. You will then see what different providers are offering.

- Type a post into LinkedIn: 'Can anyone recommend a good sales trainer for <insert job function>?' You will get many suggestions from those you are connected to. It is like turning a spotlight on in the jungle: you will have a swarm of names before you can so much as blink.

- Take those names and look up reviews of the trainers or training companies. Or watch some videos of the presenter or sales approach of the training company.

By the time you actually approach a company you will most likely have already established what they can do, read reviews and seen what their competitors have to offer. This is the ZMOT in action and it is happening more and more in B2B buying situations. Research by the CEB in 2015 (Krausova, 2015) highlighted that corporate buyers are typically 57 per cent of the way through the buying process before they engage suppliers.[2]

What the availability of knowledge means for the sales process is that companies need to expect their customers to already have a clear expectation of what service they require and what they will need to pay before they discuss potential solutions with providers. So says Dan Pink in his book *To Sell Is Human* (2014).[3]

Value of the application of knowledge

While knowledge in itself may not have the same value it once had, is there still value in how knowledge should be applied to an individual or company situation? The answer is, of course, yes, although that value is not as strong as it was in the past. There are some key disruptors that have affected the value of 'applied or executed' knowledge. They are:

Disruptor 1: Technology

Automation is currently the largest disruptor of technically complicated tasks that were previously carried out by companies selling B2B services. You can now manage your own pension and you can self-invest without having to speak to another human. Small businesses can manage their finances and post tax and VAT returns all within a single platform such as Xero or Quickbooks. If I want to write a last will and testament, I can use a template, fill in the blanks and, hey presto, for £20 I have completed a task that would once have cost £400 for a lawyer to perform.

We are already seeing the commoditization of technology services, such as the inbound marketing and sales software company, Hubspot, giving away free access to their CRM tool as a lead generator for their higher value marketing tools. This is great business for them but bad news for those CRM providers that just do CRMs.

The late, great, Professor Stephen Hawking is quoted as once saying 'The automation of factories has already decimated jobs in traditional manufacturing, and the rise of artificial intelligence is likely to extend this job destruction deep into the middle classes, with only the most caring, creative or supervisory roles remaining.'[4]

Hawking is certainly not the only person highlighting the increasing role of AI. At the end of 2016, Mark Carney, the Governor of the Bank of England, gave a speech in which he talked about the imminent 'great disruption' to the jobs market due to technology.[5]

A 2015 report by the professional services organization, Deloitte, also focused on how automation is changing the face of business and workplaces. *From brawn to brains: the impact of technology on jobs in the UK* predicts that 35 per cent of UK roles will be automated in the next 10 to 20 years.[6]

As an example of this in action, one of the 'big 4' accounting firms is already planning for the majority of audit work to be carried out by artificial intelligence by 2025.

The challenge for leaders today is imagining what parts of their traditional service will be automated and then planning for either replacing those revenue streams or profiting from the automation process itself.

Disruptor 2: Alternative services

Technology has enabled alternative service providers to disrupt the established service offerings offered by traditional service providers.

It has also accelerated the number of these new entrants to the marketplace. Two examples of successful alternative service providers are fiverr and elance, both of which give companies direct access to a wide range of skills. Or there are companies such as lawbite. co.uk, who have reworked how small businesses buy legal services.

Alternative service providers have completely disrupted the recruitment model. For instance, if a company chooses not to use an agency, it still has ready access to a pool of candidates. It has access to fixed price recruiters, to applicant sourcing services, social media tools, job boards and CV database platforms, all of which allows the hirer access to the same people as if they had gone down the recruitment agency route.

What these alternative services do is prioritize the transactional service (CVs in the case of recruitment) over perceived high value services, such as face-to-face meetings and regular contact over the phone. This provides a significant challenge for traditional companies such as accountants, lawyers and recruiters.

Disruptor 3: Insourcing

Lastly, technology is making it much easier for companies to insource services that they used to outsource. This is hoovering up much of the work that traditional professional services companies used to provide, work that enabled them to achieve good margins because it was carried out by lower level staff. For example, internal recruitment teams no longer need to pay agency fees to find them candidates that they can easily find themselves on job boards. Or marketing functions no longer need to be outsourced because technology has enabled companies to manage their own advertising, SEO, creative design, social and content marketing execution. The marketing industry is an ever-changing and still fast-growing industry, so there is currently room for both external agencies and internal departments to co-exist. In 10 to 15 years it may be a very different story.

The value of peace of mind

A large element of the traditional 'value' of a B2B service provider was based on the relationship between the professional and customer.

That relationship brought peace of mind to the customer that the right thing was being done at the right time. However, there are a few drivers that now undermine this feeling in the mind of the client.

The rise of automated solutions and alternative service providers means that customers can now see the difference in price between solutions based on the level of service they require. The result? Customers can make the choice of whether or not to pay the premium for the traditional service.

If you look at the example in Table 1.1, you can see how the industry around providing investment advice has fragmented to lower-cost or alternative solutions where individuals pay for the level of service they want. You can see that as the price increases the level of human intervention increases.

Our increasing trust in virtual solutions is affecting the way companies buy services. When Amazon and eBay launched in 1995, many people were reluctant to trust a company selling online. Fast forward to today and how much has changed: you probably shopped for, and maybe even bought, your mortgage, insurance and car loan online. You probably applied for your credit card and driving licence online too. In fact, when was the last time that you actually stepped into a branch of a bank?

Table 1.1 Cost service comparison in investment management

Buying Pension Investment Advice		
High Price and High Relationship	*Discretionary Fund Management* Where an individual's portfolio is managed by a dedicated individual, the relationship involves regular portfolio review meetings and active dialogue when required	3.0% PA charge
Mid Price and Mid Relationship	*Portfolio Management Service* Where an individual's investment funds are grouped together with other individuals' funds. This larger pot is then actively managed. The relationship involves initial consultation, annual review of the fund's progress and phone Q&A support	1.5% PA charge
Low Price and Low Relationship	*Self-serve SSIP platform* Where an individual manages all their own investment research, decision making and execution	0.5% PA charge

From a corporate perspective it was not long ago that companies felt they needed to have their own servers on premises even when there were cloud options available or software applications that were hosted on their own servers. This was because they trusted their own capability to deliver a service or to keep data secure more than cloud providers. But if you now track the growth of Amazon web services, or SaaS companies like salesforce change is happening at breakneck pace. In fact, Bain & Co predict that Cloud computing will grow from US $180bn in 2015 to US $390bn by 2020.[7]

Twenty years ago we were wedded to the notion of trust going hand in hand with a physical relationship with another human. Now our trust is placed in brands and their technology. Think about the whole concept of Airbnb: you put your spare room on a website, strangers view your room, book to stay and turn up at your door... amazing. In the face of this, do I really need to meet with my lawyer, wealth manager, recruiter or CRM provider if I already trust a company's brand? Does this mean human interaction is dead? No. But someone has to really see value in face-to-face interaction if they are going to commit the time and pay the premium associated with it.

The value of inertia

The final pillar of value for companies that provide B2B services is the inertia associated with change. The historical tendency has been that if a buyer has a supplier and they are happy with the service they are providing, then they are unlikely to proactively seek other solutions. They might even not be open to hearing about other options. The fuel for this inertia has been the personal relationship between the buyer and their service provider. The common quote would be 'They know us and what we do, so it is too much hassle to change providers.' However, this standpoint is being undermined by three marketplace changes.

Regulation

In the last 20 years, there has been no shortage of corporate scandals (Enron, WorldCom, the Lehman brothers, HBOS, RBS etc) where it has often been suggested that familiarity between the business and providers of audit services has affected the auditor's willingness or ability to report poor practices. Because of these scandals and the attendant ramifications, governments and regulators are increasingly keen for companies to be legally required to open established relationships to tender. For example, EU listed companies now need to put their financial audit out to tender every 10 years. Additional regulation concerning bribery, corruption and risk management has made companies and buyers seek to de-risk decisions by reviewing suppliers more regularly and by making the procurement process more transparent.

Rise of procurement

Whereas in the past, a manager would buy from a certain supplier because they had known them for 15 years, companies are much more sophisticated and discerning about how they buy now. There are three key drivers propelling the change.

Firstly, in more and more instances, there are multiple stakeholders involved in the buying decision. Research by the CEB in 2015 highlighted a typical decision-making group includes 5.4 buyers. Marika Krausova from the CEB said 'The challenge of this is not just the greater number of stakeholders, but also the increased diversity of stakeholders – often multiple departments, geographies, and varying levels of seniority are involved.'[8] In real life, if you want to buy some training for your team, you may need to involve your director, HR business partner, procurement and potentially other managers interested in receiving the same training.

Secondly, procurement is increasingly being elevated to 'profit centre' status because of its ability to manage costs while at the same time supporting the effective provision of goods, materials and people, as required by the business.

Lastly, line manager buyers are increasingly looking to de-risk their own buying decision preference by involving colleagues in order to avoid the appearance of any bias.

Dehumanization

The relationship between supplier and buyer is being dehumanized. This could be because of the involvement of a procurement professional, or because of a regulatory requirement, or because we are increasingly buying services virtually. Being considered a 'nice person' may still get you through the door but that might be it. Increasingly, a service is judged by others involved in the buying process and against others looking to provide the same or similar services. This means that sales professionals need to be able to articulate their solution and to articulately defend their service and pricing against other providers who look the same, sound the same and may charge less for the same.

At this point, you might be thinking I am a doomsayer walking the streets with a sign saying 'The end is nigh.' I assure you that this is not my intention. The purpose of this market overview is to summarize the challenges the professional services market faces and indeed, the challenges that pretty much every business in every sector faces now or in the near future.

The most important thing to note is that market changes will mean that any company that sells service B2B will consistently see their customers leave them for alternative service providers, automated solutions and competitors through regulated advisor rotation. Companies will increasingly be caught up in open procurement processes, a situation which will put continual pressure on margins.

In this environment, it will be more and more difficult for companies to continue to be all things to all customer profiles. Instead, organizations should consider taking a more targeted approach. The supermarket industry is the best example of how different companies build their whole business model around maximizing market share of a specific customer. Aldi and Lidl are focused on price-sensitive customers. They buffer against Tesco, Asda and Morrisons, who in turn buffer against Sainsbury's, who buffer against Waitrose and Marks & Spencer.

Companies are increasingly having to do what the supermarkets do and redefine what their core service offerings are and which type of customers they need to target.

Failure to segment your service offering and customer base can result in a mismatch between what the customer wants to pay for a service and what you want to charge. This leads to a situation where a company may end up reducing fees in order to stay competitive, thereby becoming unprofitable because they have not changed the cost model of delivering that service. Or the company may stick to premium fees but lose profitability because they are now perceived as 'expensive' and as a result lose clients. And you lose out further because you have not sought out new clients who would be willing to pay for a premium offering.

Some companies are being proactive and creating more clarity around their service offering for both staff and customers. They are achieving this by doing things such as:

- reworking existing business practices or automating services to allow a lower price delivery model;
- creating additional service lines to supplement reduced profitability of traditional high margin activities;
- working to add elements to their service that increase the perceived value in the mind of the client;
- meeting customer needs and ensuring a good customer experience to encourage them to spend more and be more loyal;
- boosting marketing and branding activity;
- adapting a proactive approach to winning new clients and retaining and expanding existing clients.

What is evident is that very few companies are doing nothing. Investment is critical to success. Whether a company restructures to build a lower cost delivery model or refocuses on finding higher value customers, both decisions involve hard work and the need to attract and retain new customers.

Whatever a company decides to do, employees need to have a clear understanding of the direction the company is going, the reason for this direction and how the goals are going to be achieved.

And this is where culture comes in…

References

1 Lecinski, J, Google (2011) *ZMOT: Winning the zero moment of truth*

2 Krausova, M (July 2015) *5 Customer Buying Trends You Can't Ignore* https://www.cebglobal.com/blogs/5-customer-buying-trends-all-sales-professionals-should-know/ [last accessed 14/4/18]

3 Pink, D H (2014) *To Sell Is Human*, Canongate Books

4 The Guardian (2016) https://www.theguardian.com/commentisfree/2016/dec/01/stephen-hawking-dangerous-time-planet-inequality [last accessed 6/6/18]

5 Carney, M (December 2016) *The Spectre of Monetarism* https://www.bankofengland.co.uk/speech/2016/the-spectre-of-monetarism [last accessed 14/4/18]

6 Deloitte (2015) *From Brawn to Brains: The impact of technology on jobs in the UK* https://www2.deloitte.com/content/dam/Deloitte/uk/Documents/Growth/deloitte-uk-insights-from-brawns-to-brain.pdf [last accessed 14/4/18]

7 Brinda, M and Heric, M (January 2017) *The Changing Faces of the Cloud* http://www.bain.com/publications/articles/the-changing-faces-of-the-cloud.aspx [last accessed 14/4/18]

8 Krausova, M (July 2015) *5 Customer Buying Trends You Can't Ignore* https://www.cebglobal.com/blogs/5-customer-buying-trends-all-sales-professionals-should-know/ [last accessed 14/4/18]

The challenge   02
of cultural change

I have always found 'culture' a fairly abstract concept to understand. However, the definition that works well for me is 'organizational culture is *the way things get done around here*'.[1]

Many individuals struggle to understand the role culture plays in their organization because culture can be such an intangible thing. For many, the most tangible interaction they have with their organization's culture comes from a 'let's make this a great place to work' initiative after the annual employee engagement survey.

The challenge that all leaders face is 'How do I bring the individuals in the company along with where the company needs to be?' Organizational change can be very hard to achieve (just how hard it can be is often underestimated). Research by the management consulting firm McKinsey&Company found that almost half (46 per cent) of financial services executives attempting company-wide digital transformation say that cultural or behavioural change is the biggest challenge facing them.[2]

The key to achieving lasting change is to go right to the core of an organization's culture, rather than just tinker around the edges. Culture goes very deep – it's how people work and how and why they make decisions on a day-to-day basis. Culture issues sit at the heart of what is sometimes called the strategy execution gap. The private research university MIT (Massachusetts Institute of Technology) has conducted research into this topic and produced several articles. Here's an example of what it has to say:

> ... to execute strategy as circumstances change, managers must capture new information, make midcourse corrections and get the timing right because being too early can often be just as costly as being too late.

This is taken from an article called *Closing the Gap Between Strategy and Execution*, published in the MITSloan Management Review, 2007.[3]

Traditionally, an organization's culture has been defined by the organization's goals. This means that organizations have not placed nearly enough emphasis on execution and getting the culture bit right. Most companies will have a strategy to grow their sales. But do they have a strategy for how to achieve that on a cultural level? Do they establish what behaviour change is needed in order to increase/change/ diverge the sales approach? Translating strategy into action is where the good are differentiated from the great. While this is a very topical issue (given the constant, unprecedented pace of change), this is by no means a new phenomenon. Books have been written on this thorny issue for years. How to translate strategy into execution is something that all organizations should be thinking very deeply about.

The traditional approach to sales transformation focuses on initiatives and tactics to improve the acquisition of new customers and the retention and expansion of existing customers. Any focus on improving culture focuses solely on the sales team rather than the culture of the organization as a whole.

Furthermore, when organizations are organized around the traditional culture model, the strategic decision-making process is centralized, with the executive team being the hub of the strategy and execution hub. In these set-ups, the executive team seeks to control 'how' the strategy is executed by both the management team and the employees. While there are many strengths to this approach, it is increasingly holding organizations back in the fast-changing marketplaces we now operate in. This is because it prevents organizations from adapting as quickly as they need in order to keep abreast of market changes. Organizations now need to be more fluid and less hierarchical, enabling strategy and execution to happen more quickly. Think back to that MIT quote – organizations have to be able to capture information and insights and react as circumstances change.

Agility is a key word here. Organizations need to be agile to keep up in today's fast-moving world. And you can only be an agile organization if you have an agile workforce. That requires a particular culture, one of openness and adaptability and with much flatter structures. It's no good if all the orders come from on high and it takes ages for insights and information to filter around a company. That's why hierarchical organizations can really struggle with agility.

Agility happens in organizations where the workforce has a voice and where insights can and are shared easily around the company, whether those insights are going from the top down or the down up. In these organizations, employees are engaged with what the company is doing, where it's going and the role that they have to play within that. Consider this quote from Aaron De Smet, partner in McKinsey&Company's Houston office and a leader in organization design, in an interview for a McKinsey&Company article, called *The Keys to Organizational Agility*:

> When you see companies that are very agile, they typically have something very special about the people and the culture that they've built.[4]

It's a lot easier for smaller, forward-looking organizations to be agile. Older, more established companies with distinct structures and hierarchies can really struggle with adapting to the agility mindset.

The biggest 'tell' of a traditional approach to organizational culture is when the leadership team does not engage with, and is not receptive to, hearing about reasons why the current strategy is not working or is unlikely to work in the future. Have you been in this situation? Almost every reader can no doubt recall a conversation with a manager or a member of the executive team where their desire for the organization to hit its goals at all costs has led to an environment where employees say what their managers want to hear rather than what they need to hear.

What are the consequences of this approach?

There are several ramifications of this approach. It results in employees often telling their managers what they **want** to hear not what they **need** to hear. In turn, managers tell their directors what they **want** to hear not what they **need** to hear. And then, you've got it, the directors tell the CEO what they **want** to hear not what they **need** to hear. This ends with the executive team and their strategy being disconnected from the reality of what employees and customers see every day. The 2008 banking crisis was in part caused by individuals telling managers what they wanted to hear, not what they needed to hear. Later in the book I talk a little about the Banking Standards Board and their goal of improving standards and behaviours in the banking industry. But linked to this point, one of the most telling questions they ask their members is 'In my experience, people in my organization are truly open to review and feedback from external sources'.[5]

While referring to the banking crisis is an extreme scenario, most leaders will have experienced this situation: you have been on a conference call during which the CEO has started shouting 'I just need you to sell more; pick up the phone and execute the basics' and all the time, you are thinking 'You have no idea about the reality of the situation.'

The CEO is angry because the numbers they see do not correlate with what they are being told. What many CEOs do not see is that they have created a culture where any answer that does not support the current strategy meets with, at best, a mediocre response.

The traditional approach is proven to help companies scale and grow in a traditional world. But in today's market, this approach makes it difficult for companies to find out about and properly understand potential market issues and to then adapt their strategy quickly enough to meet any changes in the market. This is why legacy organizations struggle to be agile.

Most importantly, in traditional companies where a poor or slow feedback loop exists between the executive and the wider organization, those companies can get stuck in a cycle whereby leaders think they have the right answers, employees know the leaders' answers are wrong, but employees do not feel they can say. This leads to poor execution, poor results, lower levels of employee motivation and more poor strategy from the executive team... and the cycle continues.

So what do we do about it?

Culture can easily be misinterpreted because many leaders see it as something that they can control and fix with a team-building initiative, a new KPI, or a new sales/marketing competition. In their eyes, culture is something that you package up and distribute.

The reality is that leaders are only able to influence their organization's culture and to influence the culture in the right way it has to be done properly. Leaders have to walk the walk and lead by example.

In my view an organization's culture is defined by three things:

- How motivated employees are to help the organization hit its goals.

- The organization's belief in how its services benefit customers and the wider world.

- How an organization chooses to treat its people. This encompasses how colleagues treat those inside and outside of their direct team, how managers treat subordinates, and so on.

The key word here is 'choose' because every employee chooses how hard they want to work towards the company's goals and how hard they want to help their customers and colleagues achieve their aims.

The HR world calls this employee engagement; a term that makes most people roll their eyes and raise their eyebrows. There are so many initiatives to improve employee engagement, but they so often fail. Gallup, the US research-based, global performance-management company, claims just 15 per cent of employees worldwide are engaged with their work (*The World's Broken Workplace*, 2017[6]). There's got to be an awful lot wrong with an awful lot of company cultures for that statistic to exist.

Instead of talking about employee engagement, I like to talk about discretionary effort. Why? Because discretionary effort reflects the actions of an engaged employee, rather than a description of the employee themself.

Discretionary effort is a term that was first coined by the public opinion analyst and social scientist, Daniel Yankelovich, and Emeritus Professor of philosophy at Villanova University in the United States, John Immerwahr, in their book *Putting the Work Ethic to Work*.[7]

The psychologist and performance management expert, Aubrey Daniels, describes discretionary effort. He says it is 'the level of effort people could give if they wanted to, but above and beyond the minimum required'.[8]

Discretionary effort implies an employee has something extra to give over and above their day job, if they choose to. This concept leads to the very important question 'What does a manager or organization have to do to encourage their employees to CHOOSE to do more than their job requires?'

This is about creating an environment where individuals **want** to do more, rather than the traditional approach of **making** them do more. It is increasingly recognized that tactics such as running sales competitions and improving compensation are not the best way to inspire discretionary effort.

How businesses can adapt to this continual change that will separate those that survive and those that thrive and the only way organizations are able to adapt is if they can bring their people with them.

Phil Jones, Managing Director at Brother UK, describes it very well: 'Customer expectation and our service delivery are attached by an elastic band. The goal of my leadership team is to ensure the business is continually moving to where the customers are and that the gap between where we are and where our customers are (the elastic) does not get stretched to the point where it snaps.'

Customers move forward now. Organizations will keep losing customers as parts of whatever it is you offer become automated or commoditized. That is an inevitable fact of modern-day business. This leaves companies with a choice: either provide a lower-cost automated or commoditized service or work harder to find new customers who do want a high-value service and are willing to pay the premium for it.

The challenge for every leadership team is that proactive business development normally sits in the discretionary effort category of people's minds. This gives leaders a puzzle to solve: how do I unlock each individual's discretionary effort and inspire them to focus it on helping the company retain and grow existing customers, while at the same time consistently finding and winning new ones?

Organizations that inspire a high level of discretionary effort from their employees will find executing a strategic change easier than those where only a minority buy in.

Imagine that every person in your organization is tied together into one big group and they are all trying to walk to a specific place. What happens if someone is walking slower than everyone else? How does it impact on the success of the overall group and their desired aim? What about if someone walks off in another direction? What about if someone moans every step of the way...? How would this be different if everyone was as excited about reaching the destination as the CEO?

Here's another scenario for you to get your head around in terms of discretionary effort. Imagine you are a wealth management company. Most of your salesforce (advisors) provide wealth management services by building relationships with customers through face-to-face meetings. Imagine that the company creates a complementary service offering, one that helps customers with financial planning. Would the current wealth manager offer existing clients access to the additional service team?

How the wealth manager acts is discretionary effort in action. Will the wealth manager do the minimum and ask their client if they want any help with financial planning (in a tone that subtly suggests otherwise). Or will they promote the service as a benefit to the client because it is the right thing for their customer, even though it will potentially dilute their own relationship with said client?

I encourage you to think of a cross-selling or cross-promotion scenario in your own organization and ask yourself what percentage of your team would choose to do more than cover the basics.

But really, do I have to do this?

The question I often get asked by clients is 'Why should I have to work at unlocking discretionary effort when I already pay people a salary and offer bonuses for them to do these things?'

The answer is because what employees want from, think and feel about today's workplace is different from what they wanted from, thought and felt about yesterday's workplace. Historically, a company's executive team would set goals and would devise a strategy to grow sales and profits then expect employees to leap into action.

However, in today's workplace millennials tend to be uncomfortable with rigid corporate structures and are turned off by information silos. They expect rapid progression, a varied and interesting career and constant feedback. Most importantly for culture, they want to work for a company where they believe in its goals and values. In other words, millennials want a management style and corporate culture that is markedly different from anything that has gone before. The companies that have already been most successful in attracting talented millennials – Google and Apple among them – are naturally innovative employers who are never restrained by 'how things used to be done'.[9]

The traditional approach to business took the view that employees are tools to be used, to have a task to complete or be moved, in the pursuit of the strategic aims of the organization. If one wanted to take a cynical view it could look like attempts to motivate employees or improve customer satisfaction are 'tactics' only deployed to support the achievement of the executive team's strategic objectives.

I appreciate that this might paint a bleak view of corporate life and that most leaders would deny that they treat customers or employees this way. However, there are a lot of employees and customers in this world who think that many companies are run with the company's interest as the utmost priority. Anything else comes second, third…

My point is that in the coming years if you think your business will need to be more agile in the way it works, or need to hire the best people to differentiate itself from the competition, or depend on employees going the extra mile to help customers, then changing your approach may well help you along the way.

This change has to be genuine though. If you say you are going to do something (being a great place to work/ caring about the environment/ paying employees properly/ doing your bit for society…) then you need to do it. Otherwise the truth will eventually out.

The organization has to live up to the values it espouses. Employees have to believe in those values or the professed culture will be very different to the real culture. Just writing yourself a good corporate social responsibility (CSR) review in your annual report and a glowing set of corporate values will not work. You need to engage with employees over what is happening and why. Workers will ask their leaders questions such as 'Why are we doing this?'

The answers that individuals receive from their managers and how they think and feel about what is happening in the workplace directly impacts the level of discretionary effort they are inspired to give.

It all comes back to how people perceive the workplace and work differently now. The very nature of the relationship between people and their work has changed in recent years: generally speaking, in the past, lots of people went to work so that they could do the things they wanted to do outside of work. Fulfilment came from extra-curricular activities. Now, lots of people want to feel that they are fulfilled while at work as well. People want their workplaces and their actions within the workplace to reflect their own values. The challenge is that, for many people, proactive business development activity often sits in the category of 'do not want to do' or 'do not feel confident about doing'.

In today's workplace, the following things need to be in place before employees will feel willing to use their discretionary effort:

- belief that the goals of the organization are good;
- belief that they are serving the interests of their customers and the wider world;
- belief that their own personal goals and values are important to the company.

Why is business development culture change challenging?

As companies look to improve their approach to business development culture there are some common challenges they will encounter.

Everyone has a role to play

Traditionally, an organization's business development culture was owned by the sales or marketing team. A challenge every organization faces is encouraging a far wider range of teams to accept and engage that they have a role to play in Business Development. At a basic level, HR, legal and operations are likely to be involved in a sales process at pitch stage. Operations and customer service are likely to be involved in identifying additional upsell opportunities in existing clients, and this is just the tip of the iceberg.

Sales team silo

The culture in many teams is typified by the phrase 'me, myself and I'. Often, sales teams have a silo mentality and operate with the attitude that everyone else is there to serve them. The job of the sales team is to win business and, once won, it is everyone else's job to deliver. This approach can lead to resentment from other teams and reduce their motivation to help them succeed.

How clients feel matters

Sales teams traditionally have been rewarded and compensated on sales made not customer satisfaction. However, in today's marketplace, **how** a service is delivered and **how** it feels to the customers are just as important as the quality of **what** the solution is that you offer. Yet in many teams we will find one person who earned high bonuses with poor customer satisfaction and see another with lower bonuses but satisfied customers. Most CEOs say they want both sales and satisfaction, but does the way you target and reward your sales teams reflect this?

A reluctance for business development

Many B2B service companies have an operating model where individuals are responsible for both selling a service and delivery of that service (marketeers, lawyers, accountants, financial advisors, investment managers, recruiters, consulting engineers etc). For most of these individuals, the act of delivering the service they have sold is more enjoyable than the active business development activity it took to win it. This means that for a lot of organizations, proactive business development activity has been a discretionary activity that is performed when the fee pipeline looks light. This can lead to companies being trapped in a feast and famine billing cycle, which is bad for business and emotional for the individual and the business. We cannot afford to be so complacent anymore.

Tension between traditional sales and digital sales

In many business development focused teams, there is a conflict between the traditional sales professionals and digital sales professionals (marketing). Traditional sales professionals believe that business development is about lead chasing, regular phone calls to clients and nurturing existing relationships. Digital sales professionals, however, believe that clients can be won and retained through social media activity and email campaigns. This creates a tension where sales and marketing teams are not collaborating to hit the collective sales goal.

The challenge is to integrate the new and the old approaches into a coherent client development approach. The two cultures need to come together.

So how do companies need to change their culture?

Just as the old proverb says a fish rots from the head down, the opposite is true when changing culture in teams. This means that change needs to start from within the leadership team.

The main changes leaders have to consider making are:

- Accept they no longer have all the answers.
- Proactively seek out the views of employees who offer unpopular or challenging insights, particularly with regards to issues that are negatively impacting on company performance. This sounds easy, but in reality it is difficult to achieve.
- Better engage with customers about what they want from an organization's service in the context of today's marketplace. Part of the challenge is for companies to deconstruct their service and allow customers to buy the bits they really want.

- Be open to engaging all levels of the organization in how change can be successfully implemented. The way forward is to trust that people at all levels of the organization have valid insights into how change can be successfully implemented.

- Improve the communication of results, challenges and plans throughout the organization.

Making these changes in your approach will be easier for some than others. In many instances you may be keen for change but know your senior leaders are not so enthusiastic.

My hope is that, whether change comes easily or with difficulty, through the remainder of the book you are able to look at the exercises and discussion topics suggested as a starting point for change.

References

1 Deal, T E and Kennedy, A A (1982) *Corporate Cultures: The rites and rituals of corporate life*, Penguin Books, Harmondsworth (reissued in 2000, Perseus Books)

2 Tanguy, C and Goran, J (March 2017) *Building Momentum for Cultural Change*, McKinsey&Company http://www.mckinsey.com/industries/financial-services/our-insights/building-momentum-for-cultural-change [last accessed 14/4/18]

3 Sull Donald, N (2007) *Closing the Gap Between Strategy and Execution*, MITSloan Management Review, MIT

4 Aghina, W and De Smet, A (December 2015) *The Keys to Organizational Agility* http://www.mckinsey.com/business-functions/organization/our-insights/the-keys-to-organizational-agility [last accessed 14/4/18] McKinsey&Company

5 https://www.bankingstandardsboard.org.uk/annual-review-2016-2017/assessment/ (Question 10)

6 Clifton, J (June 2017) *The World's Broken Workplace* (The Chairman's Blog), Gallup

7 Yankelovich, D and Immerwahr, J (1983) *Putting the Work Ethic to Work: A public agenda report on restoring America's competitive vitality*, Public Agenda Foundation

8   Daniels, A, *Earning Above and Beyond Performance* (http://
     aubreydaniels.com/discretionary-effort) [last accessed 14/4/18]

9   PWC (2011) *Millennials at Work: Reshaping the workplace* https://
     www.pwc.de/de/prozessoptimierung/assets/millennials-at-work-2011.
     pdf [last accessed 14/4/18]

PART TWO
Building a customer focus into your team

The customary starting place for a book about improving sales culture would be to focus on defining goals, followed by the strategy to execute those goals. However, as highlighted in Chapter 2, business leaders now have to think beyond an organization's financial goals elevating customer and societal benefits and giving employee values equal pegging.

The next section of the book focuses on two things. Firstly, how companies are redefining their brand purpose to better serve customer interests and engage employees who may be being asked to be involved in business development for the first time. By serving customer needs and wider societal needs, organizations are more able to engage and motivate their staff, while still delivering the financial results the business needs.

Secondly, I will show how companies are redefining their value proposition to either increase the value of their service or to shore up loyalty among existing customers.

We have already discussed the fact that one of the main challenges facing organizations is the speed of change and how it is eroding the value base of many companies. This results in a situation whereby their traditional offering is not valued in the same way by existing clients and is potentially not valued as it used to be by the customers of today.

While most companies have experienced the process of redefining a service offering, they now must get used to doing it continually due to the current pace of and continual nature of change. Companies have to keep redefining what their product is and how it serves customer needs and they need to be able to do it quickly.

Adapting to this heightened pace of change is a real challenge for organizations and sectors whose business models have been largely immune to disruption up until now. Suddenly they find they must be more agile and able to quickly adapt service offerings to customer needs.

Many companies are addressing this challenge by copying the tactics and approaches used in fast-moving, consumer-focused industries. Companies such as Unilever, Coca-Cola, Primark, Zara and so on are highly skilled at connecting with customer demand and adapting their product offering to suit consumer needs as they emerge.

Companies also need to increase their focus on how a service is delivered because the customer experience is so much more important now. For example, I had a terrible experience with a conveyancing lawyer with the result that I would neither use nor recommend him again. Recently, during a discussion with him about his dreadful service, he said 'My job is to close the house sale for you. How you feel in the process is irrelevant.' Hmm. Then there's the time when I was running a recruitment team and a consultant who was working for me received a complaint from a client about his service. The consultant put the phone down at the end of the conversation and said 'He's not very grateful. I worked hard to find him the right candidate.' The consultant clearly did not think that how a client felt was a key part of his service offering.

As business buyers become consumer-orientated in their mindset, how a company delivers its service is as important as what it delivers.

The following chapters will aim to help leaders work through the process of redefining their brand purpose and reconnecting their service offering to what their customers want and value.

Building the case for change 03

Educating and inspiring your team

KEY CHAPTER TAKEAWAYS

- Leaders need to create a compelling purpose to motivate their teams to be engaged in proactive business development.
- It is important to educate individuals and teams about why a change of approach is needed.
- It is vital to inspire people to go outside their comfort zone and engage with business development.

There was a time when sales professionals did what their managers told them to do and said what their managers told them to say! You could give them scripts that they would practise and learn. Then you sent them out to meet clients face to face for them to understand client needs and also for them to highlight how your product or solution benefited the clients' needs. Those days have gone.

The key to this approach was that you could build all your selling points into your script. The salesperson concerned would repeat it, thinking 'If this helps me earn my bonus, then I will say whatever it takes' (within the boundaries of ethical behaviour). That format doesn't work so well in today's marketplace because customers are much more aware of different service solutions and solutions are more nuanced. Scripts simply do not work because the focus has shifted away from just closing the deal. Salespeople need to have conversations with clients that don't follow a script. This can be a challenge for those sales professionals who are used to turning up, giving a presentation and walking away with a deal. A higher percentage of business development activity is now about marketing and knowing what is happening in your marketplace and why. And there is something that is more important than anything else: your salespeople need to believe in what they are selling and how it will benefit the client. Why is that so important? Because if you want your people to unlock their discretionary effort (and you do want this, believe me), then they need to genuinely believe in what they are saying, doing and selling.

Leadership teams can no longer rely on the 'This is our model, just execute it' approach; certainly not without expecting to be challenged. Do leaders realize this? Seemingly many do not. A comment I often hear from experienced sales leaders is 'I just need them to do what I pay them to do, because we know it works. I do not want to stop every five minutes and debate whether this is the right approach.'

The reality is that in today's workplace, the role of leaders is partly to sell to their teams why what they do serves the company, the customer and themselves. Only that way will leaders have workers who put in discretionary effort.

And that's not all. Leaders need people who are proactive and who know why they are selling a product or solution and what that product or solution needs to do. That means educating teams on their company's place in the market and inspiring them to find new clients and to better serve the needs of existing clients.

If you want individuals and teams to change, then they need to understand the wider context of why and how decisions are made. They need to understand the issues changes are designed to address.

Something that I am really passionate about is educating leaders about business finance. And that education needs to start early – way before they move into senior management roles. My belief is that the earlier someone understands how to read their company's management accounts, the sooner they understand the whys and wherefores of strategic decision making and the impact on the business as a whole.

I vividly remember a conversation I had with a junior manager during the recession in 2009. This particular manager was frustrated that she was not allowed to grow her team and disagreed with some of the things she had been asked to do. Rather than just tell her to get over it, I decided to teach her how to read her monthly management accounts. After an hour or so of questions and answers she said 'Well, if this is the situation, why are we not looking to remove this underperformer?' My answer was 'Because we back you to make them successful.' From then on, even if she still disagreed with certain decisions, she felt less disenfranchised by the decision-making process because she understood the wider context that we were all working in.

Think about the decisions you are currently making and changes you are trying to implement. Ask yourself 'Do those affected by the change understand the wider context of why these decisions and/or changes are being made?'

While you will have challenges specific to your own company and industry, there are some common challenges leaders of sales teams are having to address all the time. I have outlined the key ones below.

Impact of commoditization

In fast-changing markets, leadership teams might seek to reassure workers by stating that what the company has always done is the right route to take. There is a lot of sense in this approach because the 'safety of the known' is always a more comfortable place than uncertainty and lack of clarity. However, we are often moving in unchartered territory now and change is the new normal, remember. And when changing market conditions are not aired and discussed, it can affect the motivation of the sales teams. Sales teams might feel that the leadership team's strategy for success is disconnected from market conditions on the ground. They can see the change happening: they know it's there. If it isn't even acknowledged, chances are they will lose belief in the company's strategy for growth. Also, when leadership teams retreat back to the known, this approach can stifle growth, both within the leadership team and the wider organization. Sentences such as 'This is what we know always works' discourage people from thinking innovatively and questioning the status quo.

When a leadership team is more willing to discuss the impact of commoditization or changing market conditions, it makes sales professionals feel that the day-to-day challenges matter. It also helps managers match the current sales strategy in a greater level of detail to current market conditions.

Team discussion questions

- How is our market currently changing (competitors, service lines ...)?
- How is our current strategy helping us steal market share?
- How do you feel our strategy is not helping us succeed in a changing market?

Defining your target market (and communicating it!)

One of the biggest challenges for organizations is to effectively communicate where their target market lies. For sectors that are already highly commoditized (ie retail, leisure or automotive) this is nothing new. However, for many industry sectors such as financial services, recruiting, legal and accounting, this is an unknown process.

Supermarkets are a great example of a sector with players who each have clearly defined target markets. While Asda would like to take customers from Waitrose, their target customer is more likely to shop at Tesco, Morrisons, Lidl or Aldi. It has been very interesting to observe Aldi and Lidl's respective growth strategies. Their strategy has been to offer good-quality food that is competitively priced. In doing so, they are directly targeting Asda, Morrisons and Tesco customers. Would they have been successful if they had taken on Waitrose and Sainsbury's at the same time? I very much doubt it.

Many companies fall into the trap of continuing to target their whole market, rather than specific segments that match the organization's strengths, even when market conditions change. Companies need to get better at developing sales strategies that provide different delivery models to suit customer needs.

For example, in the recruitment industry, customers are now choosing a far wider range of services to help them meet their staff recruitment needs. Some are managing recruitment in-house and only use external services for niche skills. They might have preferred suppliers to manage big recruitment drives. Other customers use fixed price recruiters who search job boards and place adverts for a low fee. In some instances, companies are outsourcing their whole recruitment function to specialists. Because of this, many of the fastest-growing recruitment firms are adapting their business models to meet specific company needs. Companies such as Randstad Sourceright, Experis and Adecco are targeting the outsource market, but building a low cost delivery model that enables them to make a profit from 10 per cent margins. Others are focusing on niche skills that they know internal recruitment teams or outsourcing providers cannot source.

I can give you a great example of this. When I was working with a wealth manager a couple of years ago and we were talking about target markets, he told me 'In today's market, until you have 250k to invest and are 10 years out from retirement, you are unlikely to want to pay for my level of service!' This is an example of someone who knows their target market.

It is easy for a leadership team to outline to their sales teams where they see growth target markets. The challenge comes from adapting the mindsets of sales teams who are used to looking for 'opportunity' rather than 'the right opportunity'. This challenge is further complicated by the reality that it takes time to transition from targeting the 'whole market' to a specific market segment so, while leaders are saying 'This is our target market', sales consultants are saying in return 'Yes, but I can make money here today, do you want me to walk away?'

There is no quick answer to this retort. However, the core of the answer lies in how leaders discuss on an ongoing basis the journey from where we make money today to where we will make our money in the future.

Team discussion questions

- What are the different segments we see in our market (could they be separated on client buying behaviour, price point, service levels…)?
- Which segments best differentiate us from our competitors and play to the strengths of our current service/product?
- Which market segments are least profitable/desirable based on our current approach to business?

Scarcity of prospects

As buyers have more varieties of service and delivery methods available to them, the 'pool' of potential customers could become smaller for many companies. This is not necessarily a bad thing, but it does have implications for organizations. The first implication is that companies need to be more proactive in nurturing the potential clients they do have. With changing buyer behaviour meaning a significant part of the sales process happens before a sales consultant is contacted, companies need to work hard to be 'front of mind' at the moment a client wants to engage an external supplier.

One of the key challenges companies face is that sales professionals are often lax in adding potential clients to a customer relationship management (CRM) database and/or tagging contacts appropriately for future marketing activity. As a consequence it is harder for companies to provide the right marketing material to the right contacts, in turn reducing the likelihood that the company will get 'the call' when the buyer has a need.

Team discussion questions

- What challenges do we have finding enough **new clients** for our target market segments?
- What are the activities we could do more of to find a greater number of new clients?
- What could we do to ensure that more of the new clients we identify make it on to the CRM?

Customer churn and loyalty

Ongoing commoditization within all market sectors means the churn of customers is likely to increase. It therefore makes sense that managers need to educate and inspire their teams to make ongoing client loyalty a top priority. While most companies already focus on customer satisfaction, the new need is to focus on the likelihood that a current client will move to an alternative service provider, insource, or consolidate their supplier base.

While no firm explicitly goes out of its way to lose clients to a competitor, one of the biggest drivers of customer churn is complacency. I imagine you have some clients that have been with your firm for a number of years. They know you, you know them, it is all very comfortable. However, what is the likelihood that they are thinking of insourcing or outsourcing, or that procurement is looking to consolidate your supplier base? Do you think your competitors (new and old) are talking to them about different ways they can achieve the same outcome as your product or service quicker, cheaper or faster?

The nightmare scenario is that you get a surprise call from a client who says 'We really like what you do, but we have decided to outsource to a single provider.' The impact is compounded if you could have offered that same 'sole supplier' service. If only you had been talking to them about different ways they could buy your type of service rather than the next piece of work you will get. The challenge for sales teams is that they need to be proactive in speaking to clients about how they feel about the different service delivery methods available to them. On one hand you open the client's mind to the different possibilities; on the other you expose yourself to the possibility of losing the client unexpectedly.

Team discussion questions

- Why would we want to be proactive in talking to our clients about how they feel about the way they buy our type of service?

- What are the reasons our clients leave us to go to the competition or insource our type of service?

- Which of our clients are most likely to be interested in outsourcing, insourcing or consolidating their supplier base?
- What do we do if a client is thinking of changing the way they buy our type of service?

Repeat the mantra: We not I

The challenge that many sales directors face when trying to ensure that customers' needs are at the heart of the sales process, is that sales typically promotes an individualistic culture. Compensation plans are based on individual efforts. There is a focus on margin-generated and monthly targets, which can create a culture of short-term behaviour. This can create an environment where any change is greeted with the response 'What's in it for me?' One of the benefits of realigning your service offering so that customers are at the heart of everything you do, is that it cuts through the 'me, me, me' attitude that is so dominant in many sales cultures.

A second benefit of realigning your service offering to customer needs is that it helps to unlock the discretionary effort, particularly with regards to workers who are not directly incentivized on sales made and are not financially orientated. While this can have repercussions in the short term in terms of prompting some top players to leave, it will be beneficial in the long term. Those benefits include increased staff loyalty, higher levels of client satisfaction and, in turn, customer loyalty. Importantly, customer loyalty becomes a matter of loyalty to the organization as a whole, rather than loyalty to the single relationship they had with a sales consultant.

The third benefit is that being aligned to customer needs gives reassurance to all staff that the executive team has a plan to succeed in a fast-changing market. In all likelihood, employees will see the changes that are disrupting your market. They will be wondering 'Is my job secure? Is this organization secure? Will I have a good career here still?' You need them to keep thinking that your organization is a good place to work.

Summary

These challenges are nothing new to most of you reading this book. However, what I want you to be asking yourselves is 'Do those people I want and need to inspire discretionary effort from, understand **these things as well?** This is important because if your team doesn't understand the wider context behind the decisions the leadership team is making, the chances are that there will be resistance to any necessary changes. You need your team on board.

The overarching principle is that if you hire smart people, you need to treat them as if they are smart by explaining why you are doing what you are doing and giving them a chance to contribute their own expertise. Don't hire smart people and then treat them like idiots!

Do your teams understand your customers? 04

KEY CHAPTER TAKEAWAYS

- Customers are much more savvy now about what they want from a product or service.
- Organizations need to refocus their efforts on providing customers with what they want.
- Customer research should be carried out by the sales or service teams.
- Market research is important.
- The importance of buyer profiles and persona mapping.

The only opinions and feelings that really matter in the current marketplace are those of your customers. Look to them to find your answers. If you look at the last 15 years, the most successful technology companies have succeeded by reimagining how traditional services can be delivered and they have reimagined them around the needs of the customer. These companies have been successful because they understand how buyers view the way services work. Let's look at a few examples.

We've all found it frustrating trying to book a taxi to get us somewhere, right? It's 11pm and you've had to ring three, maybe four taxi firms to find one that can take you where you need to go, when you need to go and even then, you are never quite sure whether it will arrive or not. And then, Uber came along.

Here's another one: in the past financially savvy investors were frustrated that they still needed to speak to a stockbroker when they already knew what shares or funds they wanted to buy, and they would have to pay £30 for the privilege. Enter online trading, with Hargreaves Lansdown transforming the UK marketplace.

And lastly: jobseekers in the 1990s had the option of reading the local newspaper to find a job or registering with an agency, both potentially frustrating experiences. This frustration was the catalyst for job boards, which in turn heralded the arrival of the job search engine, Indeed. No more checking five or six job boards for vacancies. However, jobseekers are still frustrated at not being able to find vacancies that match what they need, when they need it. So, the company that knows more about you than probably any other company (Google, who else?) launched Google Jobs in 2017, with Facebook Jobs following hot on its heels. Where does this leave Indeed, the job boards and recruitment agencies? Time will tell but it won't be long before we find out.

Knowing what your customers want from your service has never been more important than it is today. For some companies, this is second nature and it has always been that way: fashion, retail, fast-moving consumer goods and automotive industries are all adept at manufacturing products to meet specific consumer demand. There's Audi, for example. Every year Audi flies thousands of people from all over Europe to Germany to look at different aspects of car design. Why do they do this? To establish what their customers think of features that will potentially be incorporated into their cars and into their competitors' cars. Sound like a fun bit of research to be involved in? I have participated in this research and it is four hours of one-to-one interviews in which you give your views on front grills, door handles, seats etc. What has stuck with me from this experience is that, for car manufacturers, no detail is too small when it comes to building a car that people want to buy.

There are two challenges for sales leaders. The first is summarized by the two questions 'How well do you know what your customers want from your service?' and equally important 'How well do you know what they like about your competitors' services (both traditional competitors and disruptive competitors)?' The second challenge is 'Who are your indirect customers?' Increasingly procurement, HR and other stakeholders are significantly involved in the buying process, although not necessarily a direct beneficiary of the service. In the case of procurement, they control the buying process and are increasingly influential in who gets selected to pitch and wins the business. The default response by sales professionals is to bypass them. Short term this may work, but long term it can significantly impact your ability to retain and grow accounts. We will talk more about procurement shortly; however, for the moment I ask 'Do you treat procurement (and others) as clients and do you know as much about them as you know about your existing customers?'

You may well be thinking 'Of course we do. We know the answers to all those questions.' Maybe you do, but when was the last time you asked your sales team for their opinions? And when I say 'ask', I mean ask in the real sense, as in seeking open and unfiltered feedback about what your sales people feel is good and bad about the service you deliver. You must have an open and receptive mind to what feedback you might receive.

How does improving customer understanding increase employee motivation?

What's the connection between having a better understanding of your customers and employee motivation? Involving the wider sales, marketing and service delivery teams can help motivation and unlock discretionary effort in a number of ways:

a) Engagement

When you employ smart people to deliver smart solutions to clients, they usually have a good understanding of the value of their own service. They know what frustrates customers and what helps them. The likelihood is that they are sharing these insights with their managers, which may or may not be going down well with those managers. Rather than viewing such behaviour as disruptive, try to harness it to cascade the insights further and facilitate a greater level of motivation for the whole team. If you engage the whole team in contributing to the process of better understanding client needs, you are more likely to inspire them to be part of the solution and implement strategies that come out of your research.

Team discussion questions

- What do you think our customers think of our service offering?
- What could we do better meet customer needs?
- What should our approach be to grow sales, profits and/or market share?

---

b) Purpose buy-in

When teams are on the hamster wheel of selling and delivery, it is easy to become disconnected from the wider purpose of your company's service. I know this from my own experience. As a recruiter, I remember sometimes meeting over 10 jobseekers in a week and speaking to another 60 or 70 over the phone. There were times when I could hardly remember my own name, let alone the needs of the candidates I was meeting. Fortunately, I had a manager who kept reminding me why I was doing all this activity, how it helped me reach my goals and how I helped others reach their goals. Therefore, as a recruiter, I lived by the mantra of 'I help people get jobs.'

When you engage your team in better understanding the needs and wants of your customers, they are more likely to believe in helping the organization deliver on its brand purpose.

Concept applied

An example of purpose buy-in is the energy supply company, OVO Energy, which disrupted the big six energy companies on its journey to supplying 700,000 UK households with energy. The big six were historically known for treating customers poorly. OVO Energy's founder, Stephen Fitzpatrick, had a founding purpose of 'customer first everything else second'. The organization's employees set themselves some rules, which were:

i)   Find a way.

ii) Be the good guys.

iii) Build something great.

Their early success was built on the foundations of building their processes around things customers disliked about the existing suppliers. This led to them building a special customer support team to help with the switching process and to not using teaser rates to attract new customers in. To help keep the customers' needs front of mind, every employee spends one day a year in the customer service team helping customers with their switching challenges.

Team discussion questions

- How do we help our customers achieve their goals?
- How does a poor service from us affect them achieving their goals?

c) Product offering

The better you know your customers, the better you can design your services around what customers need and want. This sounds obvious but is still worth saying… again and again. And the better you know your customers and design services for them, the more you are helping your sales teams feel motivated about promoting your products. Why? Because their belief level in the product will be higher. Most people fear being thought of as selling false promises, so the greater the match between customer needs and a product's features, the greater the level of proactivity you will inspire on the part of sales teams.

There's another benefit here that sounds just as obvious but still needs to be said (because it is often overlooked) and it's this: the better your product is, the easier it will be to inspire everyone within your organization to actively promote it to their networks.

Team discussion questions

- Which aspects of our product/service best meet our clients' needs?
- What aspects of our service do not benefit our clients' needs?
- What aspects of our existing service offering could we create new products / service lines around?

d) Marketing and sales strategy alignment

Whatever your size of company, be you small, medium-sized or large, it has never been easier to find and reach out to niche buyer profiles and exploit this to the max. Yet in many companies there is a disconnect between what sales and marketing see as a 'target customer'. The more insight you have on different buyer profiles, the easier it is for marketing and sales teams to align their focus on the same thing. Once sales and marketing teams are aligned it is easier for the sales and marketing processes to become more integrated, and both teams to collaborate more through the sales process.

Team discussion questions

- How well do our sales and market strategies align?
- What are the things that the sales team could do to help marketing better understand client needs?

How to approach learning more about your customers

A quick fix to understanding your customer is to get your marketing team to either conduct or commission external research about your customers.

However, client research does not necessarily need to be conducted by an external researcher. Customer insights data may already exist within your organization in teams such as marketing or customer service. An alternative option is for you to conduct your own customer research.

The challenge when conducting your own research is that unless you are an experienced marketeer or have a research background, it can be difficult to craft good questions that are free from bias.

All is not lost though! I have found a solution and it is one I have used myself, as well as with my clients. It involves using a simple framework that enables managers and companies to objectively solicit feedback and opinion. The model I have used for several years now is the 'Stop, Start, Continue, Change' approach to gaining feedback. It is an excellent approach to stimulating open conversations with individuals and groups. This type of approach exists in a number of guises. The best way I have seen it used and described is by Mike Morrison, learning and organizational development specialist at RapidBI, a team of organizational specialists. Morrison suggests that there are four aspects of feedback that are needed. They are:

1 **Stop:** What are the things we need to stop doing because it affects… ?
2 **Start:** What things should we start doing to improve… ?
3 **Continue:** What is working at the moment that we should keep doing to help… ?
4 **Change:** What is working to some extent but needs to change if we are to help… ?

The aim of each of these questions is to open a dialogue, enabling the individual or company to receive feedback openly and objectively.[1]

Another thing to consider when you set out to gain more customer insights is that you need to have clear goals of what insights you want to receive. The more specific your line of questioning the more likely you will get insights into areas you feel are impacting your growth. In addition, the more focused you are in the areas of insight you seek the easier it is to explain to your teams why these customer insights will help the organization meet customer needs better.

External research conversations

If you look at the examples below you can see how you can use the 'Stop, Start, Continue, Change' framework to plan customer research questions. A few examples follow below.

Problem: Pricing challenges

1 **Stop:** Which aspects of our service should we stop doing because they add little value to you?

2 **Start:** What could we add to our service that would increase the value of our service?

3 **Continue:** What do you value about our current service that we should do more of?

4 **Change:** What should we change about the way we work that would increase the value you see in our service?

Problem: Visibility of client buying behaviour

1 **Stop:** What aspects of our service do you think you will stop buying in the next 24 months?

2 **Start:** What services could we start to provide that would help you with these problems?

3 **Continue:** Which aspect of our service currently most helps you achieve your goals?

4 **Change:** How could we change our service to better help you with your future challenges?

Please bear in mind that this is a very simplistic approach to customer research. However, it can also be used to great effect for internal research conversations.

Internal customer research involves asking different teams about their own perceptions of customers' needs, wants, likes and dislikes. While at one level these opinions are more subjective, they are generally founded on real life experiences. The 'Stop, Start, Continue, Change' approach to questioning might seem like an overly simplistic discussion framework, but it could increase the levels of engagement in your teams as you are giving people the chance to share their frustrations and concerns about a particular topic in advance of you saying 'Now the issues are on the table, how can we overcome them?' It is important to talk about any problems before launching into the potential solutions because providing a platform for people to express frustrations before you discuss plans lowers the barriers to new ideas.

Below is a guide to how you can use the 'Stop, Start, Continue, Change' approach to plan and conduct internal research conversations.

Internal research conversations

If you are arranging meetings to solicit opinions from internal staff, you can use this approach to plan how you will set out the context or goal of the conversations. For example, if you want to improve client loyalty, you may plan your feedback conversation like this:

1 Problem/Needs to be addressed:

– Improve client retention.

2 Attendees:

– Customer service and sales team.

3 Discussion plan:

– Stop doing: What do we need to stop doing to improve client retention?
– Start doing: What could we start doing that would improve client retention?
– Continue doing: What are we doing well that is helping customer loyalty?
– Change what we do: What can we change about what we do now that will improve client loyalty?

Here's a sample of other problem areas that could benefit from this approach:

Problem: Pricing challenges

1 **Stop:** What aspects of our service can we stop providing because they do not add value it?

2 **Start:** What are the things we could add to our service that our clients would value and be willing to pay more for?

3 **Continue:** What aspects of our service do our clients value most?

4 **Change:** What aspects of our service could we improve that would increase a client's feeling of value?

Problem: Quality of service delivery

1 **Stop:** What should the service delivery team stop doing that is negatively impacting clients?

2 **Start:** What should the service delivery team start doing to make a positive impact on client service?

3 **Continue:** What good things should the service delivery team do more of?

4 **Change:** What aspect of the service delivery process could the service delivery team improve?

There are lots of ways that you and your team could use this approach, according to your needs. The challenge is getting your team in the habit of continually using this approach. They need to keep looking for more information about clients, finding out how they feel about your service. As a leader, your role is not only to build confidence that gaining client knowledge (both good and bad) is a good thing, but also to have mechanisms in place so you can track this knowledge and use it to craft better solutions/products and to support future marketing strategy.

Before we move on let's talk about procurement

At the mention of procurement it is likely that many sales professionals will roll their eyes and be thinking 'Oh, the guys we try to ignore and work around.'

I have been there as well… ducking and diving, trying not to get caught until the line manager commits and procurement can no longer influence the buying decision. I am not saying this does not still work but it is getting harder and harder to achieve and, increasingly, taking this approach will impact on your ability to win future business.

Just as in the 2000s accountants expanded from traditional accounting to commercial support across the whole business, the same goes for procurement today. Increasingly procurement are more than just buyers, they are seen as a way of achieving a strategic advantage over competitors. This means that they are often involved much earlier in a buying process and in some companies at product development stage.

The long and the short of it is that they are not going away. The reality is that for many sales professionals they are a bona fide client, whose needs and interests need to be understood and met.

Procurement has become a client group that you need to plan to build a relationship with. Importantly this means you need to conduct research to understand what they want from potential suppliers and how they expect suppliers to act in a procurement process.

This represents a significant mindset shift for many traditional sales consultants because procurement have a totally different set of interests and needs to line managers who buy services for their own teams.

I am aware you may know your clients, but I ask you to reconsider whether you know the needs and interests of all 'clients' involved in the buying process.

The best insights I have received on the role of procurement in a sales process were from Peter Belsey. Peter was for 25 years a consultant for Huthwaite International (the originators and home of SPIN Selling). His insights are based on the extensive research that Huthwaite International conducted over many years and his first-hand experience observing the increasing importance of procurement in the sales process. His advice for sales professionals when dealing with procurement is:

Tactics to deal with procurement

Approach 1: Don't pretend you can avoid them: If you know they will be involved and you want a long-term relationship you need to engage.

Approach 2: Build line manager relationships pre-tender process: If you enter a buying process at the tender stage led by procurement, they will likely stop you having line manager contact. Focus on building line manager relationships pre-tender process.

Approach 3: Be proactive with procurement. It might seem counter-intuitive but, by building relationships with a procurement team pre-tender process, this means as a tender process starts you will already have an understanding of the needs and wants of the tender process owner.

Approach 4: Create individual value propositions: create a value proposition that specifically matches the needs of each stakeholder in the tender process, including procurement.

So where does all this research and customer information lead you? Many sales teams are unsure of what to do with all the information once they have gathered it.

The idea is that, with all this information, you are in a stronger position to clarify or redefine the value of your service to your customers and how you deliver that service. You can then structure your business development strategy around proving you can deliver what you say you can.

The companies that manage this best are those that use buyer profiling, sometimes known as persona maps, across both sales and marketing teams. Persona mapping and/or buyer profiling is the process most marketing teams go through when building a marketing strategy. Many readers may already be familiar with persona mapping/buyer profiling. Persona mapping is the creation of realistic but fictional profiles of target customers, including characteristics such as goals and motivations. Buyer profiling is when you create a description of the kind of customer you want to attract.

Successful business development strategies in today's market are highly integrated with the marketing team. What you don't want is a situation whereby the marketing team has a clearer idea of who a typical target client is than the sales teams on the phones.

While understanding clients' needs is not new to any sales professional or marketeer, the speed of market change means it now needs to be updated regularly and relying on what you know customers wanted 3, 5 or 10 years ago could leave you disconnected with what your clients need or want today.

The upside for organizations that do focus on seeking customer insights on an ongoing basis is potentially higher levels of engagement from their employees. The premise is that if employees in the sales, customer service or operational teams feel their views on customer needs are actively sought or they see the organization actively listening and responding to customer feedback, they are more likely to believe the organization genuinely cares about customer needs. This belief will help unlock that discretionary effort.

I do, however, acknowledge that I have only just skipped across the surface of a topic that has many books written about it in its own right. My favourite book on this subject is *See, Feel, Think, Do* by Andy Milligan and Shaun Smith.[2]

References

1 Morrison, M (May 2016) *Stop, Start, Continue, Change Management Model* https://rapidbi.com/stopstartcontinuechangemodel/ [Last accessed 14/4/18]

2 Milligan, M and Smith, S (2008) *See, Feel, Think, Do: The power of instinct in business*, Marshall Cavendish Business

Creating a compelling, company-wide value proposition

KEY CHAPTER TAKEAWAYS

- Building a value proposition is much more than just a well-crafted statement. It is about the organization understanding how its product or service meets the customer need, making them feel that it is of value.
- Teams need to understand the different elements of the value proposition.
- The actions of teams can add, or detract, from perceived client value.

If you are a company that is providing a unique service or product, or one that delivers a significantly different benefit to your customers than your competition, how customers feel while you deliver your service is less important. This may sound odd (and controversial) but it's true. Why? Because consumers are willing to accept a certain level of dissatisfaction because of the perceived benefit of your service. Not convinced? Think about when flat screens initially hit the market. Back then, many people were willing to accept inferior picture and sound quality because of the extra space their new flat screen TV gave them. The consumer's desire to get back to the CRT quality TV has, to a large extent, driven the development of HD, 4K screens and the growth of sound bars.

Now think about Ryanair's approach to customer service up to 2013. The airline's chief executive, Michael O'Leary, was famously quoted as saying 'Germans would crawl over broken glass bollock-naked to get low fares.' It often seemed that the airline was quite happy to dispense with good customer service because the main aim was to squeeze as much money as possible from customers. Did it harm the company? It grew to be one of the largest airlines in Europe.

In a mature market where there is little difference between the range of services delivered by companies, it's a completely different story. Then, how a customer feels about an organization's service or product can be the deciding factor in a buyer's decision-making process. One of the most high-profile conversions on a customer-centric approach has been Ryanair. In 2013, the airline began to put customer satisfaction at the heart of its growth strategy. Now, customers can get an allocated seat, they can bring a second carry-on bag... Customer service has moved up the priority list and suddenly Ryanair has started taking note of what customers wanted. Just as importantly, it is taking note of what its competitors are offering.

Why is this important? Because it affects sales growth and profits. When you are a disruptive player in a price-sensitive and low-loyalty market, how customers feel does not have to be your primary concern. However, when a market has matured and your competitors have caught up with you, or you are competing against alternative delivery business models, customer satisfaction becomes a lot more important if you want to attract new customers and retain existing customers. While you might think Michael O'Leary woke up one morning and decided to make his company a nicer one, the reality is that other forces were at work – such as BA and easyJet having changed their offerings in order to directly compete with Ryanair's earlier differentiator (price). This meant that when passengers could purchase flights from BA or easyJet at the same price as Ryanair flights, they were likely to switch airline. Did Ryanair's changed business model hit its profits? Quite the reverse. Instead, its increased customer focus contributed to profits growing from €522m in 2014 to €1.31bn in 2017.[1]

The key learning point from this example is that companies need to continually review their product and service proposition to ensure that they are still giving customers what they want and that their competitors are not eclipsing their unique selling point. Otherwise, they are likely to find that profits and growth are being squeezed. Although in Ryanair's case they may well have moved to become more customer-focused in their external approach, their well-publicized flight cancellations in late 2017 due to a shortage of pilots shows they may not be taking the same approach with their internal staff (but let's leave that for another book)!

Some of you are, no doubt, working for companies that are disrupting traditional markets. However, I suspect that most of you work for organizations in mature markets with a broad competition base. While retail, fast moving consumer goods and leisure sectors are used to rapidly changing consumer tastes, many traditional industries are not. For those organizations, the speed of change has challenged not just their business models, but also their confidence in their value proposition to clients. This accelerated pace has precipitated a significant shift in how customers perceive the value of products and service. This, of course, has also precipitated a change in loyalty and the price customers are willing to pay. Some affected organizations are very aware of this and are striving to change their mindset. The mindset in today's market needs to be one of engaging the whole organization with the challenge of balancing the service delivered with the price a customer is willing to pay.

If a firm lacks clarity of its value proposition or has a value proposition that is disconnected from what customers want, sales consultants will find it harder to be passionate about their service and will struggle to promote the advantages of using them over the competition. This is something that organizations need to be mindful of.

When I meet a salesperson, I always ask the question 'You do the same as <insert competitor company>, why are you different?' The quality of their response tells me all I need to know about how well their company actively promotes its product and service proposition internally to help its salespeople externally. You may want to ask this question of your own sales team. The best answers I get show that the sales professional has a detailed understanding of their competitors' products. They are often able to define the specifics of what it is that they and their company do that means a better service for customers. The worst responses involve general phrases such as 'We are more consultative' or 'They are expensive.'

How do you think your team would do if you asked them 'Why do we represent better value to our customers than <insert competitor name>?'

What role does the value proposition play in today's market?

The term 'value proposition' is credited to two people: Michael Lanning, formerly a consultant at McKinsey&Company and Edward Michaels, director of people and professional development, UK & Ireland at McKinsey&Company. In 1988, they wrote an internal paper titled *A Business Is a Value Delivery System*, which emphasized 'the importance of a clear, well-articulated "value proposition" for each targeted market segment'.[2]

Typically, in organizations a value proposition is crafted and then disseminated for the sales team to use. However, the challenge with this approach is that defining perceived value from a customer's perspective is, at best, based on customer research (see previous chapter) and, at worst, it is based on guesswork. I think Huthwaite, in their 2017 report titled *How to Create and Capture Value*, described defining value perfectly when they wrote 'Like beauty, value is in the eye of the beholder.'[3]

As with any theory or idea, there are always competing theories or ideas about what makes the perfect value proposition. While summarizing the value you bring to your customers in one sentence seems an appealing idea, my feeling is that the real value to a customer comes from all the little things your product does and how you do what you do. I am sceptical that a single statement can encompass everything that makes a product or service of value to a customer. This is because of several reasons:

- One size does not fit all: Just as Internet marketing is increasingly able to show us adverts that are specific to our needs, sales professionals need to be able to tailor their value proposition to individual customer needs.

- Standing out in the crowd: How do you really differentiate between two accountants, lawyers, marketeers or recruiters? The reality is that at a practical level most service providers look and sound the same. A well-tailored value proposition that is matched to a client's individual needs is increasingly all that separates providers in a pitch process.

- Price: Buyers have never had so much visibility on prices charged by different providers. This means that price needs to be a more explicit part of any 'value'-based presentation. Importantly the relationship between 'price' and 'value' is not as simple as cheaper equals more value. In many cases something being cheap can actually negatively affect a buyer's perception of value.

- Hiding the bad news: In the old days it was possible for companies to ignore bad reviews or limitations of their service as it was unlikely that their customers would have had access to that type of news or review. In today's market clients have access to reviews of your service and, in all likelihood, content specifically comparing your service to a competitor (normally a disruptive start-up); just type your company name versus a competitor's name into any search engine and see what comes up.

As companies can no longer rely on the scripted, one-size-fits-all approach, they need to educate their teams to be able to match your organization's value builders to individual customer needs. Importantly there needs to be a move away from a 'value statement' and a move towards a 'value discussion' with a client. Here the sales professional discusses with a potential buyer, not only an organization's 'value builders', but also the things a company does that are 'value detractors'. In addition, they need to be able to do this while also taking into account the pros and cons of a competitor's service.

What is the customer value equation?

Like beauty, value is in the eye of the beholder.[4] (Huthwaite)

As with many things involving marketing and customer perception, there are competing views of what contributes to perceived value from a customer. The area of behavioural economics is the subject of a significant amount of research and authors such as Dan Ariely provide fascinating insights into how consumers make seemingly irrational buying decisions.

However, since the aim of this chapter is to help you and your teams better understand how to articulate the value you bring to your customers, I will try to simplify matters and leave behavioural psychology for another day!

When I work with teams I tend to break how customers perceive value into two components: firstly 'value builders', things about your service or price that add to a customer's perceived value of your service; and secondly your 'value detractors', those aspects of your product or service that lower a customer's opinion of the value of your service.

This means that when calculating a customer's perceived value, the following formula applies:

Perceived value = sum of value builders less sum of value detractors

Including 'value detractors' in the equation is important as perceived value is based on customers' perception. It may be that you have a perfect product or service that does everything a client wants. In all likelihood, your product or service has things you do well and things you do not. In my opinion one of the failings of sales training of the past is that it focused too much on 'what problems we solve for the customer' and not enough on 'how we do not do what the customer wants'. Often this leaves sales and marketing teams unequipped to engage with potential and current clients in an objective and balanced way. Some of your limitations you will have to accept, others you can work on; however, be sure that if you are not aware of your limitations then your customers certainly will be and they will be talking to your competitors about them. Working on the principle that 'forewarned is forearmed' I actively encourage you to engage your teams in what you do that detracts from a customer's perceived value of your service.

What are the components of 'perceived value'?

One of the challenges sales professionals have when looking to understand more about what customers value about their service is that they tend to focus on the functional benefits of their service above all else. In part this is because most sales professionals are trained to identify customers' functional needs and promote their service against these needs.

A typical sales conversation will go like this.

Sales Pro: 'Mr Customer, could you tell me what problems you have with <insert functional area or project>?'
Client: 'This system/campaign/project is not working well and we are running over budget and will miss our target.'
Sales Pro: 'I am sorry to hear that. Let me outline a couple of features of our service that can help you get what you want.'

While slightly oversimplistic, it shows how sales professionals work as a default. It is not a new problem and people like Neil Rackham have been working to solve this problem with SPIN selling since 1988.[5] More recently the CEB (now Gartner) have promoted the 'challenger sale'[6] as a solution to sales professionals being too one-dimensional in how they promote their services.

To the credit of SPIN selling and the challenger sale, they do encourage the sales professional to look beyond the 'functional' benefits their service brings. SPIN explicitly encourages conversations with clients on the 'implications' of a particular problem not being solved. The challenger sale advocates a different approach, where the sales professional becomes an 'educator' where they build trust and credibility with the client. However, both approaches have limitations when it comes to establishing a customer's 'perceived value of a service'. To this end when working with teams on 'perceived customer value' I am more explicit in outlining the drivers of perceived value.

The four main drivers behind a customer's perception of value are:

1 **Functional benefits:** How does the product or service help the customer achieve their desired aim?

2 **Customer satisfaction:** How does the delivery of the service feel to the customer?

3 **Customer brand affinity:** Does the customer have affinity towards the company's brand?

4 **Price:** How does the customer feel about the price they paid in exchange for the solution and service they received?

While the traditional value equation of **Customer Value** is Benefits–Cost (CV=B–C) does talk about the outline perceived customer benefits, I feel it is not explicit enough in the component parts of what 'customer benefit' means.

I prefer to break 'customer benefit' into the three component parts: functional, customer satisfaction and customer perception of company.

You can see from Figure 5.1 how, rather than a see-saw in the traditional 'customer value' equation, I advocate a sliding scale where 'value builders' raise perceived benefit and 'value detractors' pull down perceived benefit.

The premise of this approach is that everything a company does pre-sale, during service delivery and post-sale contributes to our perception of value. For example, you buy a new pair of shoes and, although you love the shoes, you had to wait ages in the shop to find a sales assistant willing to help you. The shoes were priced the same in other shoe shops. When you add together how you feel about the shoes, the service and price, do you think you got value? Would you return to that shop as your first port of call again?

In a professional setting, many companies are investing significant sums of money producing white papers, running events, supporting charities and so on, with the goal of creating a positive brand affinity with customers. The goal is that at the point of need, customers and potential customers will call them first or that customers will be more willing to accept a higher price or be more open to advice from sales consultants.

This is so important for sales teams as it requires sales professionals to think more broadly about customers' perception of value. Sales teams need to focus on syncing their efforts with their marketing team and on being more marketing-centric in their approach, rather than focusing on closing the deal.

This can mean that if you are in a market where your buyers are aware of your competitors' service, their perception of value will be influenced by what your competitors do or do not do. As I clarify each of the value drivers in more detail, be conscious that for each driver, customers will be measuring you against how your competitors are

Figure 5.1 The customer value scale

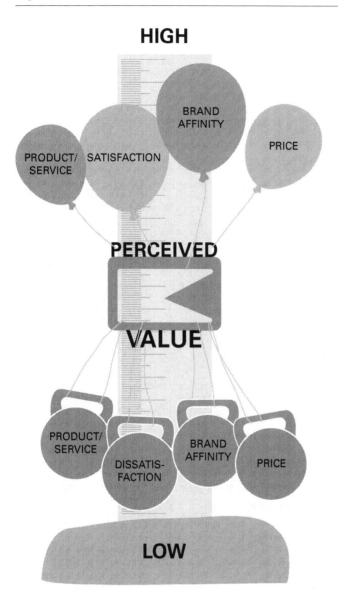

performing and what they are offering. Also, in situations where you come out the same, the perceived value lessens.

Below is an overview of each of the areas of perceived value in more detail and an exercise for each that you can conduct with your team.

Product/service value

This is the benefit the buyer gets from you having successfully delivered your product or service. This is often the definition of 'value' that many sales professionals understand best. When a company sells a physical product, it would be how effectively it executes its intended function. In the case of anti-virus software, for example, it would be how well it stops viruses and hacks. For a recruitment firm it would be finding the right candidate; for a financial advisor, suggesting funds that grow ahead of the market; or for a marketeer, a campaign that generates a significant number of leads. The key here is that the more competition you have in your market, the more likely it is that your clients will be directly comparing your service against services they have already bought, which in turn means their perception of value will be more finely tuned than a customer who buys a service for the first time.

Let's take the Uber example. It delivers a taxi service, something that has existed for decades. However, Uber now delivers a better product than traditional taxi firms and has transformed the taxi-booking experience for millions of people that are, in many instances, happy to pay a premium through Uber's surge pricing.

Exercise

Below are a few examples of value builders and value detractors. Can you add three value builders and detractors of your own? (Advanced: can you add a stat of measure to prove you do these things?)

Product/service value builders

- We solve XYZ problem.
- Delivers functionality XYZ promised.
- Improves efficiency by X%, productivity by X%.
- Reduces costs by £XX, down time by XX hours.

1

2

3

Product/service value detractors

- Less efficient than competitors.
- Less functionality than competitors.
- Only solves part of the client's problem.

1

2

3

Service satisfaction

For most companies in today's marketplace, what makes them different from their competitors is not 'what' they do, but 'how' they do what they do. Increasingly customers perceive value according to how they feel during the delivery of your service. A real life experience would be to go to Aldi or Asda and ask a member of staff where you could find tomato ketchup. You will probably be given an aisle number and then left to find it. Then go to Waitrose and ask the same question. No matter what the staff member is doing, they will walk you to where tomato ketchup is displayed. This discrepancy is not because the staff are nicer or better at Waitrose than the staff at Asda or Aldi; it's a specific example of how Waitrose differentiates its service and generates a higher level of perceived value. Just as I have compared Waitrose and Asda/Aldi, so will your customers compare how you do what you do against their experiences with your competitor.

Exercise

Below are a few examples of value builders and value detractors. Can you add three value builders and detractors of your own? (Advanced: can you add a stat of measure to prove you do these things?)

Satisfaction value buildings

- Customer feeling listened to and understood.
- Seller doing what they said they would do.

- Handling complaints or concerns well.
- Adapting the buying process to reduce customer inconvenience.

1

2

3

Dissatisfaction value detractors

- Customer feels they are not listened to.
- Complaints or concerns handled badly.
- Finding the right person to speak to is difficult.
- Blaming others when things go wrong.

1

2

3

Company or brand affinity

The third driver of perceived customer value is the 'affinity' a customer has towards the brand. While marketing has always cared about brand reputation, for the rest of the organization it is a relatively new thing. Partly because customer affinity towards a brand is quite difficult to define, but also, and probably more importantly, the way brand perception spreads is word-of-mouth and / or based on PR distributed by the company. In today's marketplace where social media rules, bad news about a company can spread significantly faster than PR departments can manage. Consumers are also more likely to base their brand perception on what they hear from within their social networks. This change impacts many sales teams because in today's market 'how' they, their colleagues and organization act pre-sales process, during sales process, during service delivery and post sale, will impact a potential client's perception of a brand and the perceived value associated with it. This is another example of where a 'consumer mindset' is infiltrating the business-buying process.

Exercise

Below are a few examples of value builders and value detractors. Can you add three value builders and detractors of your own? (Advanced: can you add a stat of measure to prove you do these things?)

Brand affinity value builders

- Company running thought leadership events.
- Brand reputation built over time.
- Providing high value marketing content that helps clients solve problems for themselves.
- Sharing free insights or advice to clients who have challenges you could help with.
- Going beyond contractual requirements post sales to address client issues.

1

2

3

Brand affinity value detractors

- Sticking to the letter of contractual obligation.
- Lying about a situation or conversation.
- Poor employee reviews on sites like glassdoor.
- Negative social media posts.
- Only being interested in speaking to people when there is money to be earned.

1

2

3

Price

Frustratingly, price and perceived value is the most important driver to articulate and master, in large part because how clients view price and value is not always logical, rational and is, in many instances, inconsistent. The price of a product or service can both positively and negatively impact perceived value. What makes price and perceived value unusual is that low price can be both a value builder and detractor, just as high price can be a value builder and detractor. Sounds weird, right? Many people will have seen a product and thought 'That seems too cheap to be any good.' This negatively impacts perceived value. Equally, many of us will have seen an expensive product and thought 'Well, it must be good if it costs this much.' In today's market the challenges companies face is that high visibility of pricing between different providers means that sales professionals need to be more willing to openly discuss pricing and the different physical and intangible components that go towards supporting their price.

Exercise

Below are a few examples of value builders and value detractors. Can you add three value builders and detractors of your own? (Advanced: can you add a stat of measure to prove you do these things?)

Price value builders

- When you deliver the same product in the same way as your competitors but cheaper.
- When you offer extra features or benefits as part of buying your service.
- Offer extra rebates or guarantees on product or service.

1

2

3

Price value detractors

- Charging more than competitors for exactly the same service.
- Being unable to explain how you do what you do to justify your price.
- When you charge the same for a lower quality service (ie digital delivery vs face to face, customers do not understand the work involved in delivering a service).

1

2

3

In the exercises above I made suggestions on what your 'value build-ers' or 'value detractors' could be. Only you will know your business well enough to know what those things are that will add or detract from the value of your service in the mind of your customers.

Putting the theory into practice

In the previous chapter we spoke about researching your custom-ers and internal staff to get an understanding of things you could start doing, stop doing, continue doing and change about how you work. The reason that exercise works with your teams and custom-ers is that it is simple for people to understand what is being asked of them. It's possible to transfer the answers you get into the value perception model. This can help you take a long list of opinions and help the leadership, sales, marketing and operations teams under-stand how customers perceive their value.

The exercises below are designed to use with your team to turn the ideas on paper into words that they can use with clients. The exercises range from the simple to the complicated. By doing this, your sales team gets to practise the things they should be doing. Even more powerfully, the managers will get to see how well each person in their team can articulate how your service or product matches a customer's needs.

Value mapping exercises

Exercise

Easy exercise: Map your value builders and detractors

Learning objective: Encourage your team to understand the aspects of your current service that add value or detract value from your service.

1 Using the value perception template (see above), managers need to get their teams to map the features of their service and map the value builders and the detractors that influence buyers' perceptions in each of the four areas.

2   Ensure that the group is proactive in entering detractors of your service or product offering.

3   Close the discussion by asking 'How does this collection of value builders and value detractors change how we pitch our service to clients?'

Exercise

Medium/difficult exercise: Map value builders by comparing yourself to your competitors

Learning objective: Educate the individuals and managers in a team on how well they know how you differentiate your service from your competition.

1   Using the value perception template (see above), managers need to get their teams to map the features of their competitors' service and map the value builders or the detractors against each of these four areas.

2   Ask the team to prioritize the competitors' features that they feel create the biggest obstacle for you to overcome when presenting your solution to clients.

3   Open a discussion by asking the following questions:

    –   How do our service value builders help us compete against the competitor strengths we have highlighted?
    –   Where does our service proposition need to improve to overcome these competitor advantages?

FAB selling exercises

While it's an old school approach, FAB selling is still as relevant today as ever. While it doesn't explicitly help close more sales, it is central to keeping sales professionals focused on the problems they are solving for the client, thus building value in their product or solution. In short, FAB stands for:

Feature: 'Because it has… '

Advantage: 'You will be able to do… '

Benefit: 'This will help you… '

In real life it might look something like this:

Personal example

Product: Mobile phone

Feature: Finger print scanner.

Advantage: My phone is more secure. It is quicker to log in.

Benefit: This means I save time logging in which means I can spend more time...

Business example

Company: Buffer (social media posting tool)

Feature: Automated posting of social media content.

Advantage: I only have to stop once in the week to fill my 'bucket' with social media content for the coming week.

Benefit: While I am travelling in the week delivering training and attending client meetings I am still actively marketing my business which helps me grow sales.

Exercise

Easy exercise: Feature, Advantage, Benefit

Learning objective: embed the practice of attaching product or service features to specific client needs.

1 Ensure participants have a sheet of paper divided into three columns, with each column having a heading of 'Feature', 'Advantage' or 'Benefit'.

2 In the Feature column, get participants to write down two or three of your service or product features that add value to a client.

3 In the Advantage column, add the advantages that each feature brings the client.

4 Next to each feature and advantage, write the Benefit you think the client or company will receive from this particular feature. (Note: Benefits need to be something that helps them personally rather than functionally, so should be things such as 'X problem will not happen, which means you will hit your deadline every month...' '... save you time...' '... hit your target...'.)

> **5** Now for the tough part. Get each person in your team to stand up and present to the team a FAB statement they have prepared. Judge them not on the power of the feature, but how well they connect the feature to the benefit the client will receive.
>
> You may think this is a straightforward exercise. However, having run this exercise with hundreds of sales professionals, I can tell you that you will be amazed at how many drift off when it comes to the benefit section of the statement, leaving clients to work out for themselves how a product or service will benefit them.

Once your team has mastered the first FAB exercise, they will be ready to take things to the next level. The statement will now be slightly different as it starts with a restatement of a defined client need. This means the statement is now a NFAB statement:

Need: You said you need XYZ.

Feature: XYZ is a feature of our service that can do this.

Advantage: It will help you by...

Benefit: Which means that you will solve XYZ need.

A statement may look like this:

Need: You said that you dislike being rushed during the pitch process.

Feature: What we do at the start of a pitch process is agree a timeline for each aspect of the pitch process to ensure you hit your implementation deadline.

Advantage: You get to work at your own pace and will only receive a nudge from us when it looks as if you will miss your implementation deadline.

Benefit: You will enjoy the process as you will not be hassled by us. But at the same time, you know someone is focused on helping you hit your implementation deadline.

Exercise

Medium difficulty exercise: Matching client need to FAB statements

Learning objective: Participants can start to connect needs or problems their clients may express with features of their product or service. Importantly, they can vocalize how their service attributes meet client needs.

1   In preparation for this, you need to write sticky notes for all the different difficulties or challenges you know your clients have. Fold each sticky note up.

2   Let each person in a team pick one sticky note from a hat. They then have four minutes to create a NFAB statement that shows how your product or service features can solve the client's problem.

3   Get each participant to present their NFAB statement to the rest of the team. (Note: the team should be judging on how well the feature meets the needs identified on the sticky note.)

4   Ask the remaining participants what other features they may have highlighted to meet the initial identified need.

Summary

The 'value' of a service has always been difficult to pin down. However, in today's fast moving marketplace, companies and teams need to be continually thinking about how their service offers value to all the different types of customers they sell to. Everyone involved with the business development process needs to be able to articulate a service's value and, importantly, individuals need to be confident and capable engaging in a dialogue with clients about what they perceive as 'value'. The key to this last part is helping everyone in the organization regularly practise value-based conversations. Which is where I hope the exercises in this chapter can help you.

References

1 O'Shea (June 15) *Ryanair: Good manners give profits a lift-off* http://
   www.pressreader.com/ireland/irish-independent-weekend-review/
   20150606/281535109603359,[last accessed 14/4/18]

2 Golub, H, Henry, J, Forbis, J L, Mehta, N T, Lanning, M J, Michaels,
   E G, and Ohmae, K (June 2000) *Delivering Value to Customers* http://
   www.mckinsey.com/business-functions/strategy-and-corporate-finance/
   our-insights/delivering-value-to-customers [last accessed 14/4/18]

3 Curran, J and Huthwaite, *How to Create and Capture Value* – global
   research report http://horizons.huthwaiteinternational.com/creating-
   and-capturing-value-global-research-report/ [last accessed 14/4/18]

4 Curran, J and Huthwaite, *How to Create and Capture Value* – global
   research report http://horizons.huthwaiteinternational.com/creating-
   and-capturing-value-global-research-report/ [last accessed 14/4/18]

5 https://www.amazon.com/SPIN-Selling-Neil-Rackham/dp/0070511136

6 Dixon, M and Anderson, B (2012) *The Challenger Sale: How to take
   control of the customer conversation*, Portfolio Penguin

Streamlining the 06 buying process throughout your business

KEY CHAPTER TAKEAWAYS

- The sales process has changed dramatically in the past 10 years. It is no longer about a sale being made, but about helping customers to buy.
- A new mindset and collaboration are key to succeeding as a modern-day sales professional.
- The B2B sales process is similar to a retail process.

My first job in sales was a Saturday job as a teenager working in a sports shop in the centre of Bristol, selling tennis rackets. When interviewed for the job, I was told I would be given all the training I needed to succeed. The first lesson I learnt was that you always need to question what your colleagues ask you. How so? On day one I was sent to the local hardware store to ask for a 'long weight'! After 20 minutes I twigged. The reality was that I only received one training session from my manager, but it was a good one and remains one of the most useful sales training sessions I have ever received. In fact, it is the foundation of my approach to selling that I still use today. And as I will explain, it is increasingly important in the approach of today's sales professionals.

My first sales training went something like this:

Manager: 'Alex, today we are going to talk about how you sell lots of tennis rackets.

Me: 'Great, I am ready.'

Manager: 'There is only one thing you need to know and remember. You are not here to sell things but to help people buy the things that they want.'

Me: 'OK, so what does that mean in real life?'

Manager: 'When you meet a customer, your job is to:

1 find out what they want and why they want it;

2 show them things that will give them what they want;

3 ask them what they think;

4 go silent.'

Me: 'I think I can do that. Anything else?'

Manager: 'No, that is it. Just remember, your job is to help people buy what they want, not sell them things they do not need. Congratulations. You are now qualified to work in retail! Remember your job is to help people buy.'

While over the years I have learnt many other approaches to selling and closing deals from sales gurus and authors such as Neil Rackham, Joe Girard, Tom Hopkins, Zig Ziglar and many, many others, this first lesson was still the most formative. It is increasingly the approach that many other sales professionals are also taking.

Nowadays, the role of the sales professional is increasingly similar to the role of the assistant buyer, as found in the retail industry, rather than the 'deal focused closer' more typically associated with someone in sales. I am not for one minute suggesting that B2B organizations need to become retailers, but I do think the parallel is useful because the way B2B buyers are making purchasing decisions increasingly resembles how we buy as consumers. The good news is that you and your teams are already expert consumers. You already have insights into how your clients' buying process is changing and now need to tap into those insights and create plans to match your processes to those changes.

Figure 6.1 Differences between traditional B2B sales process and retail sales process

Retail sales process	Marketing Team					Sales Team
Customer buying process	Aware-ness	Interest	Consider-ation	Intent	Evalu-ation	Purchase
Traditional B2B sales process	Marketing Team		Sales Team			

Let's look in more depth into the growing similarity between retail organizations and the B2B sales environment.

One of the biggest differences with a retail environment is the role marketing plays in the sales process. Figure 6.1 above represents the typical stages of a customer/client buying process.

As highlighted in Figure 6.1, in the retail environment the role of marketing is to not only gain interest in a product, but also help the potential buyer through the 'consideration' and 'intent' stages of the sales process. The result of this is that by the time a retail buyer enters a store, the role of the sales assistant is to help the potential customer evaluate the options open to them and ask what they would like to buy. You might be thinking that this approach is great for selling shoes or clothes but not relevant to your organization.

The challenge with the traditional approach is that, while companies might want to maintain the status quo, clients do not. Even as far back as 2012 evidence was starting to mount that B2B buyers were progressing through more of the buying process before engaging with a sales professional. IDC's 2012 IT Buyer Experience study reported that an average of nearly 50 per cent of the purchasing process for technology solutions is complete before a salesperson becomes involved.[1] Roll forward to 2018 and B2B buyers' comfort level in researching and considering is only getting greater. The question for you is 'Has your sales process adapted to help your potential clients self-serve themselves through your sales process?'

What this means from a practical standpoint is that as traditional roles of marketing and sales change in the customer buying process, the roles of sales and marketing teams need to change as well.

Figure 6.2   Differences between traditional B2B sales process and modern
sales process

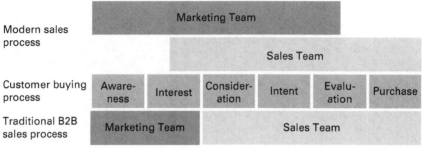

You can see from Figure 6.2 above a representation of a modern sales process showing a significant overlap between the role of the sales and marketing teams.

This area of overlap has been called 'smarketing' by Hubspot, but is more commonly called the area of 'sales and marketing fusion'. However, these moving boundaries between sales and marketing are creating a number of challenges. Firstly the need for sales and marketing to collaborate, secondly the need for sales teams to take a more 'marketing'-centric approach and lastly for marketing departments to think more about how they can help across a wider range of the sales process.

In summary, as business to business buyers become more 'consumer' orientated in their buying behaviour, sales and marketing teams need to adapt their approach to help potential buyers through the sales process in the way they want. The remainder of this chapter is focused on helping you review and adapt your sales process to ensure it matches how your clients want to work.

So... the good news

The first bit of good news for your business development culture is that moving to a marketing-centric approach to business development is a lot more appealing for people than asking them to 'sell more'. What would individuals in your customer services team rather do? Focus on value-add client conversations over a few weeks then call and show them some extra options they could use to help them OR make a call to a buyer they do not know, to say 'We have this product, would you like to upgrade?' In short, it gives purpose to many of the customer service/marketing-related activities you promote your teams to do. This is because rather than being 'nice to dos' they are an explicit part of the sales process: namely, helping a customer feel like they want to buy from you rather than you feeling like you need to sell to them.

The second piece of good news is that many people in your sales teams are already doing this. Take a look at your sales teams' business development activity. What percentage of their time is spent pitching for specific deals? How much time is spent nurturing relationships with internal stakeholders, buyers and influencers, just to get the opportunity to pitch at some point in the future? The reality for many sales professionals today is that they spend more time on marketing-based activities, building credibility and trust with a potential client, than they do actually pitching for specific deals.

This marketing-centric approach creates a problem for many businesses with traditional sales processes because their expectation is that sales professionals will focus their efforts on clients buying now, rather than sales professionals working to be front of mind when the client's need arises. What this means is that there needs to be a shift in mindset, both on the part of business leaders and sales teams. The focus needs to be on sales professionals being a more integrated part of the overall marketing strategy, rather than the deal closers.

I hope that my thoughts on the sales process needing to focus on helping people buy, rather than focusing on closing the sale, works for you. As I run through some of the things you can do within your teams to adapt current thinking and behaviour, I hope you also see how helping people buy is more likely to help engage the discretionary effort your teams have to give.

Switching from a 'selling' mindset to an 'assistant buyer' mindset

Getting your target clients to want to buy rather than being sold to, has always been much easier said than done. Moving from a 'selling' mindset to a 'buying' mindset is an enormous task and worthy of a book in itself. So to simplify matters, I am going to focus on things leaders can do to improve how different teams collaborate to design and execute a single coherent sales process with the single aim of helping current and potential clients buy more. Each area will have a short description followed by an exercise that can be run with a single team or across multiple teams.

1 A silent struggle for power

It can be fair to say that when it comes to the relationship between sales and marketing, the sales function has been the dominant player in the last 50 years. However, this is changing. As more and more of the sales process is taking place before a buyer makes contact with a company's representative there is an increasing reliance on a marketing first approach to the sales process. In 2006 Philip Kotler, Neil Rackham and Suj Krishnaswamy wrote about 'ending the war between sales and marketing'[2] and described how 'each group often undervalued each other's contributions'.

Roll forward 12 years and the sales landscape has been totally transformed; social media and the digitization of many industries means marketing plays an equal if not more important role in the sales process. In many instances sales teams are being replaced by a purely digital sales process; this is particularly evident in new tech start-ups/digitally native organizations where the goal is to grow sales and there is no established 'marketing silo' or 'sales silo'. In many other companies the marketing team is becoming an integral part of the sales process right through to a buyer's evaluation of different options open to them. In addition sales professionals are spending more of their time in 'client nurturing' type activities typically associated with marketing. However, through speaking to numerous CEOs, sales directors and marketing directors, the frustration Kotler, Rackham and Krishnaswamy highlighted is still evident. The phrase I liked most was written by Ben Firman, CEO of 80–20 Growth Corp, where he said that 'sales and marketing groups exist in a state of cooperative competition'.[3] Which, in reality, can switch from cooperation to passive aggressive compliance and finger pointing in quick time.

The heart of this silent struggle for power is the two functions working to align their competing strategies to grow sales, budgets and resource allocation. The situation was best described to me by Nick Lee, a professor at Warwick Business School, who said 'Sales feel they own the customer relationship whereas marketing feel they own the whole organization from the brand downwards. They often feel that the sales team corrode long-term customer relationships.' In the end the power struggle comes down to both sides wanting to be the dog and neither wanting to be the tail!

Exercise

This exercise has two parts. Firstly, to bring out into the open any disconnects between the sales function's perception of its role in the sales process and the marketing function's role in the sales process. The second part of this exercise is to bring into the open frustrations or challenges each function has with the other.

Aligning sales and marketing leadership

Ask each person in the discussion to answer the following questions, placing each answer on a sticky note:

- **Stop doing:** What should we stop doing that impacts how sales and marketing work together?
- **Start doing:** What should we start doing to improve how the sales and marketing teams work together?
- **Continue doing:** How do sales and marketing teams work together well already?
- **Change what we do:** What could we do to improve how the sales and marketing teams collaborate?

Ask participants to put their sticky notes in one of four places on a wall or table (Stop, Start, Continue, Change). Then facilitate an open discussion around the areas that are most relevant and important to the team.

2 Aligning sales and marketing processes

Building on the point above, the chances are that your marketing team has a structured process to deliver a stream of leads to the sales team. The sales team in turn has a structured process for nurturing those leads until there is a definitive buying opportunity and then a process for managing a pitch or tender process with a client. As the diagram above infers, the 'flip' between sales and marketing is a single event within the process.

However, as buyers change their buying behaviour, sales cycles lengthen, and the increasing diversity of solutions open to buyers will mean that relying solely on a marketing approach or solely on the sales team will probably not deliver the results needed.

This means that it is increasingly important that a sales process supports both sales and marketing teams being involved through the whole sales process. This is more than marketing having their plan and the sales team having theirs. The key is that a company's sales process is just a single sales process where the marketing and sales teams have responsibilities to support the potential client through the process and the other function executes its responsibilities.

A great example of an integrated process was a recent experience I had with the inbound marketing and sales software company, Hubspot. I downloaded a white paper and an hour later I received a call from a salesperson, asking me to book a demo; more importantly he knew which white paper I had downloaded. In fact his opening gambit was focused on why I was interested in the white paper topic. While booking the demo the salesperson was asking qualifying questions to ensure the demo focused on my specific needs. I had the demo and said 'Not now thanks, I will stick with my current marketing platform.' Since then there has been a seamless flip between sales and marketing and I have received emails that specifically focus on helping me get more value from my existing platform and highlighting Hubspot features. As a lead nurturing process, it integrates sales and marketing, while also being tailored to my specific situation. You might think that Hubspot is good at this just because it is a CRM company. However, after trying another couple of platforms, I could see their sales process did not actively integrate the marketing and sales functions, as Hubspot did.

The key to this case study is that while my experience did not make me buy, it certainly has made me a 'fan', meaning that I am much more likely to recommend Hubspot to friends and peers who ask for a referral. A question for you is how many non-buyers leave your sales process as 'fans'?

Exercise

Aligning the sales and marketing teams and the sales process

The goal of this exercise is to encourage both teams to see the sales process as one process which they both are collectively responsible for, rather than 'my funnel' and 'your funnel'.

Step 1: Preparation

- Three different coloured sticky notes.
- In preparation for this exercise, replicate your sales process along one wall using sticky notes. (The goal is that your teams can see your whole sales process from initial contact through to post-sale service and account management.)

Step 2: Activity

- Using sticky notes ask participants to write down what actions need to be completed at each stage of the process. (Use one colour note for marketing, another for sales and another for operations (if you want to go that deep).)

Step 3: Discussion

- Ask 'In which areas do responsibilities overlap?' and 'How well do the teams collaborate at these stages of the sales process?'
- Ask 'In which places could the process be improved if marketing and sales supported each other more?'

---

3 Adapt the sales process to mirror a client's buying process

A traditional approach to the sales process was to keep in touch with a potential client, assuming things were business as usual until there was a change in circumstances that caused them to have a need.

At this point you would focus all your attention on getting yourself an opportunity to pitch for the business.

But as has already been highlighted, clients in today's marketplace now have more options to solve problems internally. They also have a far greater awareness of different types of solutions available externally. When this is added to a more complicated buying process, life becomes harder for the traditional 'lead chaser'. This means that when a potential client has an issue that needs resolving, they are less likely to look immediately for an external solution, as they would have done in the past. Instead, they might do nothing. They might seek out an internal solution or if they do go externally, they will consider a wide range of solutions and it is likely that they will have agreements in place to determine who they pitch to first.

This makes it harder to rely on 'hot lead' chasing or just promoting your solution when a client in your network has a need. In all likelihood, the sales professional has to track a potential opportunity over a longer period of time as a client first tries to work through the problem by doing nothing, then by using internal resources or different external providers before considering other options.

This process will vary from company to company; however, what you can see in Figure 6.3 below is a simple flow chart of how a customer's buying journey may work.

Starting on the left you have a client in 'business as usual' mode, then 'BOOM' a change catalyst occurs that means a client has to review and decide on the different options open to them.

What this mean for the sales professional is that if a client decides to do nothing, they need to track whether 'doing nothing is working for the client'. If doing nothing does not work, the client may then choose an internal option such as seconding resource from other parts of the organization. Importantly the sales professional needs to be able to do this without being seen to pester the client. What it also means is that, in this 'watching' phase of the sales process, marketing may be able to support the 'nurturing' process or customer service teams.

The key is that each team knows their role and knows the client behaviour they need to see to trigger a 'flip' to another player in the sales process. The art of this process is for the company to be close

Figure 6.3 The customer buying journey

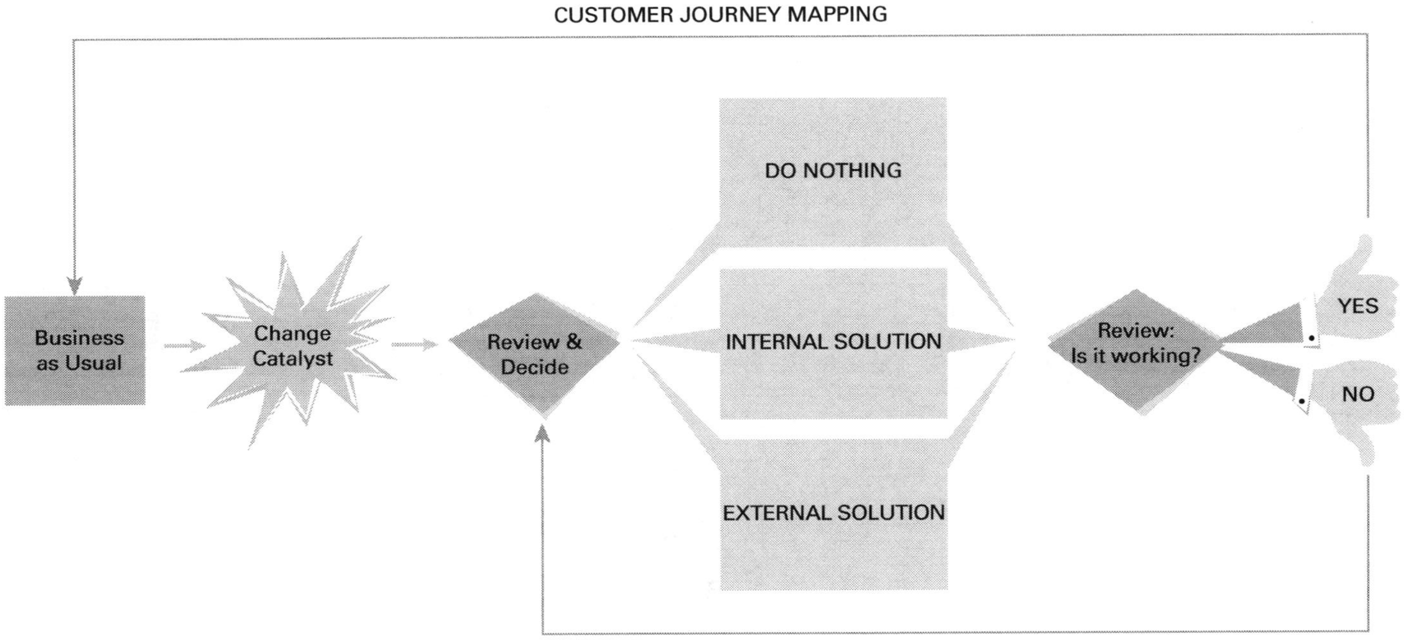

CUSTOMER JOURNEY MAPPING

enough to the buyer to show they 'care and can help' but not so close that they seem to want the client to fail in their current approach.

If the client does decide to use an external solution the next step for the sales professional will vary depending on whether they are a preferred supplier or whether their solution is already an accepted option within the organization. For many sales consultants who are not on preferred supplier agreements or are selling an alternative solution to the established norm, they may have to nurture the leads while existing external options are considered and rejected.

This means sales professionals need to be more patient than ever before and they need to focus less on winning the deal and more on being the contingency plan if what the client is doing is not working. One of my first directors summed it up to me when I complained that the people I was calling either had internal options or a preferred supplier list of external providers. He said 'Alex, everyone has a spare tyre in their car so if they get a puncture they can still reach their destination. Your goal is to build a relationship with potential clients so that if one of the solutions they are trying does not work, you can be their "spare tyre" and get them to where they need to be.' In today's market this saying has never been truer.

Sales and marketing teams now must change their approach from being 'the solution' to being 'a solution that can help if what you are doing at the moment does not work'. This means that the lifespan of a lead is longer because the sales team will need to track the opportunity as the client considers and tries multiple different approaches before reconsidering. This stretches the capabilities of both the marketing and the sales teams. Marketing teams are strong on content and messaging, but they can struggle to personalize messages to individual client needs. Sales teams are strong on building relationships but can struggle with a varied approach to being 'close but not too close' to the client as they work through the options.

This is leading many companies and sales teams to look at reworking how their sales and marketing processes can mirror the buying process of their clients. Just as consumers expect ever more personalized marketing approaches, B2B buyers are also raising their expectations. However, as sales and marketing teams are not aligned, it becomes very difficult to deliver a consistent message to both potential and current customers.

If our goal is to streamline who your organization nurture's a client relationship with, let's look at an exercise that can help you engage your sales, marketing and operations teams in collaborating better.

Exercise

Aligning the sales process to the customer buying journey

The purpose of this exercise is to help managers engage their teams in defining how the sales process can mirror the customer buying journey. By doing this the manager will stimulate a conversation internally about how both the marketing, sales and operations teams need to change their approach to nurturing leads.

Step 1: Preparation

There are two possible ways to prepare:

- Firstly, write the different stages of your customer's buying process on individual sticky notes. Then stick them on a wall in the order that the buying process follows. Or:
- Secondly, use the full-page diagram of the customer buying journey (page 91) as a handout.

Step 2: Exercise

Intro: We are here today to discuss how we can better match our sales process to the process the client goes through before they buy.

Review and discuss

Get the team to review the buying process on the wall/sheet in front of you. Answer the following questions:

- How do you think this reflects the buying process your clients go through?
- What would you change to make this process more accurate?

Improve and discuss

Review the buying process on the wall/sheet in front of you. Answer the following questions:

- At which stages of the buying process is our sales process effective at nurturing customer relationships?
- Where could our sales process be improved to better nurture relationships?
- How could the marketing, sales and operations teams better nurture customer relationships through their buying journey?

4 Lets break down the silos

The last area we need to talk about in this chapter is silos. Marketing live in their silo. In some organizations, digital marketing sit in a different silo from the traditional marketing silo. The sales team sit in their silo. Teams sit within their own silo in the sales silo and, often, individual sales consultants sit in their own sales silo. Everyone in these silos is focusing on their own targets and needs.

The consequence is that, while everyone is living in their own silo serving their own needs and interests, the actions of one department can directly or indirectly impact another department's effectiveness. Silos create a number of issues, one of the main issues being that often when a sale has been made and passed on to someone else for delivery, the salesperson can 'overpromise'. They promise clients off-plan solutions in order to close the sale but end up giving the operations or implementation teams a headache delivering on promises made at the final stages of a deal. There is often a lack of awareness of how one team impacts another in this way. For example, the sales teams may hate coding contacts in the CRM because they feel they can remember without the system or have their own spreadsheets but the unintended consequences of this is that marketing now has poorer quality data from which to run their own campaigns.

Concept applied

The problem

A VP of sales at a software company described how there were significant issues between the sales team and the implementation team. The sales team was prone to overpromise or, at worst, sell a solution the organization had no capability to deliver. This meant implementations took far longer to the point where seemingly profitable multi-year contracts became unprofitable within six months of implementation.

The solution

Hold weekly pipeline review meetings between sales, implementation teams, client services, legal and sometimes HR (where TUPEing staff were involved). In the meeting potential deals were reviewed based on the scope of the project and ability of the organization to implement the contract. The key was that each stakeholder was able to raise potential issues ahead of contracts being agreed. This gave the sales team the chance to rescope the client solution or price accordingly. The VP noted that the early meetings were lengthy and largely unenjoyable as different teams learnt to work together.

The outcome

The main benefit was that improved collaboration meant that the sales team had a greater awareness of what could and could not be delivered, leading to quicker and more productive pipeline review meetings. From an operational perspective, implementations became smoother and were often completed under budget, all of which led to increased contract profitability.

There are two exercises that you can do that can help break down the silos between teams. The first is creating a common language and the second selling the value of data.

The first goal when you want to break down silos between teams is to create a common language between all sales teams, marketing and operations. Imagine a board meeting where the marketing director stands up and says 'This month's white paper on "planning your retirement" generated 200 leads' to which the sales director replies 'No it did not. You generated 200 names of people that were interested in retirement planning, but only 20 were interested in actually engaging anyone for financial planning services. It took weeks to sift through the names.' Who is right? The answer is both. The challenge is that marketing and sales often have different definitions of what constitutes a lead. Sales teams use terminology such as suspect, prospect, lead and customer, or names target companies target A, B, C or gold, silver, bronze clients. The terms sales teams use often change team to team and location to location. Marketing uses terms such as interest groups, leads and segments. It is stating the obvious but having many different terms for the same thing across an organization can make it much harder for sales and marketing teams to support each other. It can even result in customers receiving competing messages from different parts of the same company.

Exercise

What do we… ?

This is a fun exercise to bring the differences in understanding between different teams and functions across the organization to the surface.

Step 1: Preparation

Write a list of questions that highlight different situations or types of customers where you feel you need a consistent definition or understanding. If you have time, you could write multiple choice questions or statements with multiple choice answers.

Step 2: Group exercise

1 Pose the questions that you prepared earlier to the group as a whole and get them to write down their answers.

2 Compare and contrast:

   i   Gather all the people from the same team or function together and get them to compare answers.

   ii Ask individuals from other departments or teams to sit with each other and compare answers.

Step 3: Group discussion

- How consistent were the answers from the people in the same teams?
- What differences were there between the different functions?
- What are the consequences of having a consistent language?

Step 4: Group solutions

- Show a list of terms or phrases and ask the group to discuss what each one should be called. Facilitate a consensus.

Step 5: Follow-up

- Ask managers from the different departments to share their action plan in order to implement the changes.

Worked example

What do we:

- call someone who is currently giving us business?
- call someone who has not given us business for 12 months plus?
- call someone who has downloaded a white paper?
- call someone who we are actively targeting for business?
- call a client who has the ability to give lots more business than is currently?
- call someone who currently has an operational challenge we could help solve?
- call someone who can influence a buying decision?
- call someone who is an intermediary between our client and us (eg HR, procurement, IT)?
- define as a lead?
- define as a hot prospect?
- define as someone we are pitching to?

What is a lead?

- someone who has downloaded a white paper;
- someone we have met at a networking meeting;
- someone who is currently looking at buying what we are selling;
- someone with an operational challenge.

What defines a target client?

- someone who buys what we are selling;
- someone who buys what we are selling and is able to buy;
- someone who buys what we are selling, is able to buy and likely to buy in the next three months.

Your second goal is to sell the value of data. Each department in your organization will have their own view on what data is important to them. What is often missed is that data that is considered irrelevant for one team is often critical to another. Typically largest resistance to entering data into the CRM often comes from the sales teams.

In traditional sales teams, how a sales professional organized their target lists was their prerogative. However, the resistance of sales teams to enter data into the CRM is increasingly becoming an Achilles heel that inhibits performance. In an integrated sales and marketing process, all individuals and teams are aware of what they can do to help other teams succeed or provide support services.

Where sales teams enter these pieces of information in the CRM system (ie client interest tags), the marketing team can send targeted content to specifically engage that client's interests and profile. Also, marketing teams may gather client data, such as interests, from the type of content that generates a new name or be able to track articles prospective clients have read on the website. However, if this insight is not passed on to the sales teams, it will impact their ability to make a credible first call to a prospective client.

A quick question for you: how would you rate your sales and marketing teams' ability to collect, store and share data that helps the sales process become more efficient?

Summary

Traditionally companies have had a sales process, which is often accompanied by an internal language implying that potential buyers are 'pushed' through the sales process. However, if your aim is to engage a wider section of the organization in the sales process, both the language and the intent of the process need to change. While the term 'sales process' will undoubtedly stay, the key is that a sales process mirrors the buying process a potential customer goes through, rather than the process the sales team want to push them through. In many instances this change of approach will lengthen the sales process and increase the likelihood of other stakeholders such as procurement being involved in the buying process. What this means on the ground is that marketing, sales and operations teams need to be more closely aligned so when customers are actively buying, the sales team can step in, and when the client is less active the marketing team can maintain and nurture the customer relationship. Lastly and most importantly, when a potential customer becomes an actual customer the transition between sales and operations needs to deliver a customer experience that leaves the door open to further sales being made.

References

1 Murray, G, Zvagelsky, I, Schaub, K, Gerard, M and Vancil, R (2012) *The 2012 IT Buyer Experience Survey: Accelerating the new buyers journey* http://studylib.net/doc/8154771/survey-the-2012-it-buyer-experience-survey--accelerating [last accessed 14/4/18]

2 Kotler, P, Rackham, N and Krishnaswamy, S (2006) *Ending the War Between Sales and Marketing* https://hbr.org/2006/07/ending-the-war-between-sales-and-marketing [last accessed 14/4/18]

3 Firman, B (2017) *Why Your Sales and Marketing Departments Hate Each Other*, The globe and mail https://www.theglobeandmail.com/report-on-business/small-business/sb-marketing/why-your-sales-and-marketing-departments-hate-each-other/article33515594/ [last accessed 14/4/18]

PART THREE
Aligning company and personal goals

How well would you say your organization currently works? If, like many other people, you work in a company where alignment between organizational goals and the goals of the employees could be better (a lot better maybe), then this section is for you. Research shows that many CEOs are frustrated by the gap between their strategies and the execution of the strategy by their employees.

There are lots of potential reasons behind the strategy execution gap. However, there are three factors that I see potentially impacting motivation in organizations. They are:

- Employees have little or no awareness of their company's strategy or goals.

- Leadership awareness of goals is often limited to what needs to be achieved in their function.

- Managers fail to connect what an individual will gain personally if the company hits its goals.

Let's assume that everyone in your organization knows that your primary motivation is to maximize sales and profits. However, outside of knowing that the organizational goal is to make a profit, what level of awareness do your employees have of your strategy to achieve revenue and profit targets? What awareness do they have of the role that they will play in the execution of your strategy? I would speculate that once you go below the senior management level, many of your significant shareholders have a greater awareness of the organization's strategy than the people working on executing that strategy day to day. This might sound strange, but if you were to listen in on the meetings your sales managers run every week, how many would be regularly referring to how today's priorities are helping the 12/24 month plan of the organization? The likelihood is that they will be focusing on sales pipelines and what is going to be closed this month or next.

A test I often run during workshops is to ask how many of the people in the room have read their company's annual report (assuming they are listed). This is important as if individuals are not aware of your strategy and their role in helping you to achieve the strategy, then it will be harder for them to unlock the discretionary effort.

Some organizations are great at knowing where they are at and where they are going and everyone in the organization knows it too. Sports teams, for example: 'Our goal is to win the league' or tech start-ups: 'We are disrupting the <insert sector> market.' While more established businesses may not have strategies that will win a league or disrupt a whole market, there are lots of things that you are trying to achieve that, when tangibly explained and communicated, will significantly boost employee motivation levels. Entering new markets, launching new products and growing market share over your competition are a few of many strategies that can motivate staff to work harder. More specifically, if your industry is one that is being disrupted by technology, globalization or alternative service providers, then your strategy to thrive, rather than survive, will provide plenty of opportunities to unlock the discretionary efforts of your employees. It all starts, though, with them being aware of what your strategy is and why it exists.

Apart from being paid, how well does your manager know what you want out of coming to work? It could be that they know you want new skills in XYZ area, or to finish a specific qualification or to buy a house; alternatively they might not know any of this. What each person wants from their work is different, but everyone wants to feel that their manager is actively working to help them get what they want in life by doing a good job at work. The trade between 'what we want' and 'what our company wants in return' is at the heart of whether or not we enjoy our time at work. However, it always surprises me that of the 200 managers I work with every year, only

50 per cent know what individuals in their team want from work over and above money. This means they have individuals in their teams exerting high levels of discretionary effort (hopefully), but other than a bonus, their manager has little idea of the true motivations for wanting this money or how their effort will improve their career prospects. And if they fail to deliver... trust is lost and motivation falters.

Lastly, to overcome the strategy execution gap, there needs to be a more detailed process of connecting the company's needs and the individual's needs, the goal being that both the company and individuals achieve what they want at the same time. For this to happen, there needs to be a dialogue between the company, manager and individual. The annual/quarterly appraisal is the natural place for this to occur. However, it is well documented by organizations such as the professional services firm Deloitte and the CIPD (Chartered Institute of Personnel and Development) that the appraisal process doesn't work for either party: employer or employee. Many companies, including Microsoft, Gap and Accenture, have stopped conducting annual appraisals altogether.[1] An appraisal should be an opportunity for an employer and their employee to align their goals in the coming months, but it often falls short. Instead, much of the focus is on reviewing past activities and targets that were hit or not hit. Later on we will address how managers can better align their organization's needs with the needs of the individual.

The goal of this section of the book is firstly, to help leaders better understand what individuals want in return for turning up for work every day and secondly, to help managers align the interests of those working in their teams with the wider goals of the organization. Finally, I will try to show how engaging a wider section of the business in how strategies and plans are executed can increase engagement in implementing change.

Reference

1 Simms, J (2017) *We've Ditched Appraisals. What Next?* https://www.peoplemanagement.co.uk/long-reads/articles/ditched-appraisals-what-next [last accessed 14/4/18]

Do you know what your employees want?　　07

KEY CHAPTER TAKEAWAYS

- Most people turn up to work each day wanting to achieve their own goals, rather than the goals of the organization.

- An awful lot of managers don't know what individuals want from turning up to work.

- Managers need to engage in a proactive dialogue with individual team members to understand what they want from work and how to achieve it.

With some books, the title tells you all you need to know before you read it. Simon Sinek's book *Start with Why* (2009)[1] is one of those books that does that. His premise is that, for leaders to inspire action in others, they need to start by clearly defining why they think action is needed and what benefit they bring to those they serve.

We have already discussed how to approach reclarifying your service or value proposition. However, something that is often overlooked when inspiring action from your employees is that there is more than one 'why' that needs defining. In some ways, the easy 'why' is the company 'why'. The difficult 'why' to define is the 'why' for each person in your team. The reason this is so difficult is that the 'why' is unique for each individual and the 'why' can change from week to week, month to month and year to year.

Why does your team turn up to work every day? And why do leaders need to know the answer to this question? If you know 'why' your people turn up to work every day and therefore 'what' they want in return for their effort, you have a significantly higher chance of inspiring action or a change in behaviour. Think about it from your own perspective. How well do you feel your manager understands why you come to work every day? How well do you feel they understand what you want your next career move to be? Most importantly, do you feel they are helping you get what you want, as well as getting you to do what they want? Ideally, you should feel that you are in a win–win situation, with you getting what you want and the company getting what it wants in return.

You might be thinking that you do not care about whether your manager knows what you want from turning up to work every day; however, the likelihood is your team do. However, as far back as 1924 there is research that indicates work levels of productivity are higher when people feel someone is interested in their wellbeing at work. The outcome from one well-known piece of research is called the 'Hawthorne effect'. The Hawthorne effect came from research conducted by Elton Mayo, an Australian-born sociologist. He was commissioned to study the effects physical work conditions had on productivity in Western Electric Hawthorne plant. In short, over a period of time researchers changed a variety of factors in the workplace from the lighting levels to the rest breaks, one at a time. They then studied the effect on productivity each time and discussed the results with the workers. Every time they found that each change brought further increases to productivity and finally when things where returned to how they were originally, productivity was at its highest level and absenteeism had plummeted.

A key part of Mayo's findings was that it was not the changes that had increased productivity but that someone was actually concerned about their workplace and willing to discuss the impact changes had on them personally.

So what does the Hawthorne effect mean for managers today? In essence it means that showing an interest in how individuals feel at work can impact motivation and productivity. So do your team think you are interested in how they feel?

A common paradox is that while sales leaders have built a career on understanding client needs and offering solutions to help with those needs, they forget all about the foundational principle of selling (which is to understand your client's needs) when in a position of leadership. You need to remember that employees are your clients now too.

Just as a great sales professional motivates clients to **want to** buy a service or product, so a great manager motivates employees to want to do their job. You need to sell people on doing their job, particularly if they are to keep working how you want them to work when your back is turned.

When I first became a manager, I fell into the trap of telling people what to do and pushing my team to act with no questions asked, rather than inspiring them to want to act. I was a top biller and a manager to boot, so why would they not do what I said or act on what the company needed them to do? However, in hindsight, at the moment of promotion I had subconsciously forgotten everything I knew about sales. I went from being a consultative salesperson to a pushy high-pressure salesman, forcing my team to buy the ideas I was selling. After three months I was losing the war of attrition; I was so busy telling them what I thought they should be doing and what the company thought they should be doing that I overlooked what they wanted. What I should have been doing, of course, was adjusting and adapting my suggestions to align with their own motivations and goals.

For many managers, helping employees to realize their ambitions is becoming harder and harder. I was working with a group of leaders recently and when we were talking about individual purpose and goals, one of the directors shared that his dream was to open up a donkey sanctuary in Spain. You could literally see the CEO's eyes pop out of his head. It wasn't because he had just found out that this individual's main motivator was to start a donkey sanctuary, but because he realized that he was utterly clueless about the longer-term purpose of one of his key directors.

In the past, as one CEO put it, 'to motivate a salesperson all you need is a generous bonus scheme and a good company car policy'. In today's workplace, while the big bonus is still a large motivator for many sales professionals, other factors such as career aspirations, personal challenge and work–life balance are increasingly driving motivation levels. Research by the professional services firm PricewaterhouseCoopers called *Millennials at Work: Reshaping the workplace* (2011)[2] found that financial remuneration has definitely slipped down the priority ladder. The number one consideration for millennials in the workplace, according to the report, is their personal learning and development. This is followed by flexible working hours with cash bonuses in third place. Surprised? Plenty of people are.

So how well do you understand why each individual in your team comes to work and what they want from being at work? Remember, while you may have known the 'why' and 'what' 3, 6 or 12 months ago, how recently have you checked that what you know is still relevant? The reason this is so important is that the better you understand what someone wants in the short, medium and long term, the easier it is to match what you need with the benefit they will get from doing what you ask and the easier it will be to unlock the discretionary effort you so need.

Be curious

While they say curiosity killed the cat, the chances are it had a successful life prior to sticking its nose in the wrong place. Curiosity is, in my view, one of the best indicators of whether someone will be successful in sales. An innate desire to understand how the world fits together and to seek ways for the world to be better is the perfect starting point when looking to be a consultative sales professional. The same can be said for leadership. Curious leaders are interested not only in why people turn up to work, but also what things could change to help them, and others achieve their goals.

From a personal perspective, I have always been lucky to have managers that have been very curious about what I want to achieve out of work and why this is important to me. In turn, my belief that they were working towards helping me get these things meant that I wanted at the same time to help them get what they wanted (which might explain why I spent 16 years in one company). When I think about managers connecting a work task with individual goals, I am always reminded of a call from my CEO at 5pm one day. He said 'Alex, I need you to be in Guildford tomorrow to give a talk to 100 people. I know you want to be at home for a commitment, but it will help you get experience for when you want to be a professional speaker.' And there he had me. My long-term goal has always been to be a speaker, as well as a trainer and an author (tick, tick, tick, yes!). Needless to say, not only was I in Guildford the next day, but I was also excited to be there, even though it meant missing the first day of a lads' golf weekend.

So, how curious are you about 'why' individuals in your team turn up to work every day? This goes beyond asking the standard question in the annual appraisal 'What do you want to achieve over the next 12 months?'

I am often asked by managers I work with 'How do I find out what motivates Anwyn/Connor/Jack...?' My answer is typically 'Have you asked them?' While this response is a bit of a dodge, it is also the best answer I can come up with. Anyway, let's face it, unless I know the person concerned well, I am unlikely to know the answer!

A good starting point for managers wanting to know more about motivation would be read Dan Pink's book *Drive: The surprising truth about what motivates us*.[3] In his book, Dan popularizes key aspects of the motivational theory of self-determination, the key principles being that each person has three intrinsic (inner) motivators. These are Autonomy, Mastery and Purpose. Autonomy is the desire to make our own decisions, Mastery is our need to be better and better at what we do and Purpose is our desire to achieve something that is bigger than ourselves.

From a personal perspective I see one key benefit that comes from understanding the impact of Autonomy, Mastery and Purpose in motivation and this is that it helps me as a manager diagnose potential causes for low levels of motivation or performance before I address them with an individual. What this means in practice is that I can look for potential areas for demotivation before they become demotivating. For example, high levels of KPIs for experienced sales consultants may indicate a lack of opportunity for autonomy in a team.

Autonomy questions

- How important is being able to manage your own day/workload?
- Why is the independence to make your own decisions important to you?

Mastery questions

- How do you want to develop what you do at work?
- What skills, situations do you want to improve at?
- How important to you is continually developing your skills?

Purpose questions

- Why do you want to be successful at work?
- What do you want to achieve out of work?
- How do you feel work can help you get what you want out of life?

NOTE Any answer to these questions should be followed by a curious 'WHY?'.

A mistake that many managers make when asking their team members about their motivations is that they see them as a single interaction: manager asks a question, team member gives an answer, job done… That's no good. Good managers use these questions as the starting point of a wider, ongoing conversation. Just as a sales consultant will often use question funnelling techniques (when you start with general questions and then hone in on the answers, gathering more and more detail) to more fully understand a client's situation or need, the same approach can be used when engaging in motivation discussions with employees. The value in the additional detail is that it will help the manager understand why a particular goal is important. And even more importantly, the manager can ascertain how strong this particular motivator is through the passion and detail of the explanation.

Example

Question funnelling

A simple example of question funnelling is this:

Manager: What do you want to earn in bonuses this year?
Sales consultant: I want to earn £15,000.
Manager: Great, what do you want to spend it on?
Sales consultant: I want to i) pay off some debts and ii) put a deposit on a car.

This exchange is followed by:

i) Debt questions

Manager: How much is the debt you need to pay off?
Sales consultant: I need to pay off £30,500 tuition loans from university.
Manager: How much of your debt will this bonus clear?
Sales consultant: I want to clear £8,000 with this bonus and have it paid off within three years.
Manager: Why are you keen to pay off this debt?
Sales consultant: Because I want to start saving for a flat and get on the property ladder.
Manager: Why are you so keen to buy? It can be cheaper to rent.
Sales consultant: replies...
Manager: Asks more questions...
Sales consultant: more replies...

ii) Car deposit questions

Manager: What car do you want to buy? Have you test driven it yet?
Sales consultant: I want an Audi S3, but I have not test driven it yet.
Manager: How much do you need as a deposit and what will your monthly payments be?
Sales consultant: I need £4,000 and the monthly payments will be £300.
Manager: What is it about the S3 that makes you want to own one?
Sales consultant: Because I have always wanted a decent car to match the ones my friends have.
Manager: Why do you want to have a car as good as your friends? Surely it is better getting lifts in their cars.
Sales consultant: replies...
Manager: asks more questions...
Sales consultant: more replies...

Career custodian: Challenge and recognize

Whatever level of understanding you have of your team's personal goals, it does not change the fact that you are the career custodian of each person in your team. This means that you have a responsibility to help individuals in your team get what they want out of their career. This is more than just providing opportunities to succeed. It is a manager's willingness to monitor an individual's actions and behaviours and reconcile them with the individual's stated goals and motivators. Importantly, a manager needs to be prepared to recognize when behaviours and actions support the achievement of goals and to openly discuss when there is a mismatch between a person's actions and behaviours and their stated goals.

For example, you may have someone in your team who wants to be the top fee earner in your business. However, they also are known for treating customers poorly by looking for a quick sale. In this situation, a manager will have the chance to sit down and say 'You said you wanted to be number one, yet you treat customers badly, which will affect your client retention and make being number one more difficult. Which is more important here: being number one or making a quick sale?' The conversation can go lots of places from here. It could be the team member did not realize, so your focus is educational. It could be that you discover that what they want is a quick bonus more than being number one. Wherever the conversation goes, both the manager and individual will have a greater awareness of true motivators.

The premise behind this is that it is very hard for managers to make someone in their team do anything and keep doing it when their back is turned. Just as it is very difficult to make a client buy and not cancel as soon as you leave the meeting. So, the goal of managers is to encourage individuals in teams to want to do the things they need to do. When the manager takes the mindset of a career custodian, it is easier to open conversations regarding behaviours and the impact it will have on achieving an individual's goals. The conversation could typically start with 'You said you want to achieve XYZ, but you are doing this. Why do you think this is happening?'

Managers can achieve a greater awareness of someone's goals and motivators through regularly using a person's goals as the measure of their actions and behaviours. The skill for managers to master is using the right goals or motivators in the right situations.

Educate and inspire

When I look back on my time in education, I do not think I ever had one lesson on goal setting or how to get what you want. Fortunately, my summer job at university was working for a firm called The Southwestern Company, where I received a full education in goal setting and getting what I wanted. Why did they provide this training for what was essentially a summer job? It was because the fundamentals of the job involved travelling to the United States and selling educational books door to door, 80 hours a week for commission only. From their perspective, the nature of the job meant managers could not enforce hard work. An easier life as a camp counsellor or travelling the world was just a single decision to quit away. The only option open to them was to inspire individuals to work hard for 80 hours a week, for no guaranteed pay, knocking on doors and dealing with all the rejection that comes with selling door to door.

What was their answer to these challenges? They provided great sales training, but they did more than just train individuals; they invested equal time in teaching everyone to be able to self-motivate. This involved educating us to understand our purpose, educating us to create goals, to build plans to achieve those goals and most importantly, how to manage attitude through the ups and downs that come with working to achieve goals.

This leads me to ask you a question. I get that your firm probably provides extensive training on sales and business development, but how much training do you provide to help individuals self-motivate? When was the last time you ran a session on how to set goals or how to understand motivators?

Educate by finding, watching and discussing

One of the best things about the way the world works today is that there is an almost unlimited supply of great content on websites and YouTube that can help managers have effective training discussions with their teams. I've got one for you too. This exercise is a simple three-step process.

Exercise

Find, watch and discuss

> **Step 1:** Ask two or three individuals in your team to search YouTube for a video that they think is good for understanding motivations or goal setting (or pick another topic).
>
> **Step 2:** Play the video clips.
>
> **Step 3:** Discuss with your team the following things:
> - Which were the ideas that resonated the most?
> - Why?
> - Which ideas could the team implement?
> - Why?
> - What could I do (as manager) to help you put these things into practice?

There you have it, a simple exercise that will only take you as much time as you spend in the room watching videos and discussing them with your team. And you have started the process of teaching them that self-motivation is important and that they have equal ownership in learning how to self-motivate.

Goal setting practice

Goal setting can often be massively overcomplicated, so starting simple will help you and your team build confidence in the goal-setting process. Using the GROW coaching formula (see Chapter 11), this is an easy exercise to start your team setting simple goals to achieve.

Exercise

Goal setting practice!

Goal

- What do you want to achieve this month/quarter/year?
- Why do you want to achieve this?

Reality

- What is the gap between where you are and where you want to be (billings, activity volume, activity effectiveness...)?
- What skills do you think you lack that you need to get you to where you need to be?

Options

- Which areas can I focus on improving that would make the most difference?
- Where can I get the skills or advice I need to improve my capability?

Way forward

- What specifics are you going to focus on?
- Are they SMART (specific, measurable, achievable, relevant and time bound)?

Numbers and ratios

Sometimes sales teams have a plethora of numbers and metrics that they use to drive performance. The challenge is that while managers may know why each metric or KPI is important, there is often a disconnect between the leadership and the wider sales team. If you asked one of your sales consultants to explain how each of their KPI's directly contributes to their success could they do it? This exercise focuses on managers helping their team connect the metrics or KPIs they are measured by with their earning goals. You can see from the worked example below how I take a US $10k target and work that back to monthly KPIs that sales consultants can work towards.

However, managers trying this exercise should ensure that the table reflects the measures and metrics their own organization uses in the sales process.

Figure 7.1 Sample activity and effectiveness ratio sales funnel

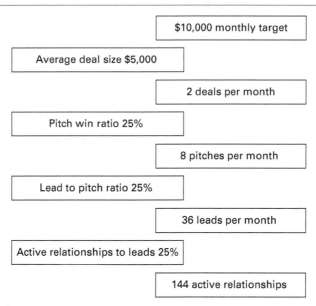

	$10,000 monthly target
Average deal size $5,000	
	2 deals per month
Pitch win ratio 25%	
	8 pitches per month
Lead to pitch ratio 25%	
	36 leads per month
Active relationships to leads 25%	
	144 active relationships

Numbers and ratios

Step 1: Manager to complete a sample table that can be used as an example during the discussion.

Step 2: Ask individuals to write down what they would like to earn in a year, quarter or month.

Step 3: Convert the earnings target into a billings or fee target.

Step 4: Help them convert the billings target into a range of metrics using ratios that help them understand each stage of your sales funnel.

Shared goals

Sometimes, as sales managers you can look and sound like a machine to those in your team. You may be caught in the trap of preaching about what the company needs and the metrics that need to be hit, while sharing very little about your own goals and motivations. I have had individuals in my teams say I sound like a corporate machine, rather than a normal human being. On reflection, it shouldn't have been a surprise that individuals in my teams were reluctant to share their goals or aspirations with me when they got little humanity from me. What I found was that the more I was willing to share my own goals and aspirations, the greater the level of sharing that I received in return. It may be that you are already a 'human' leader. However, if you think you may be a little machine-like, then the book *Why Should Anyone Be Led By You?* by Goffee and Jones (2006),[4] has some great advice on becoming more human, or 'authentic' as Goffee and Jones call it.

Pinboard motivation

An approach is encouraging team members to share their goals with each other to create a great bond between individuals.

One of the most impactful team meetings I have been part of took place one January Monday morning. Everyone was asked to bring in magazines or brochures that probably contained images of things they wanted to buy or achieve in the coming year. We then spent 45 minutes cutting out pictures and sticking them to a piece of card, which we then presented to the rest of the team. However, technology has changed the way this exercise would work, partly because people buy fewer magazines now. However, there are of course, technological replacements. It would be easy for everyone in a team to create a board in Pinterest containing things they want to achieve, buy or experience in the coming year. The best thing about this is that the Pinterest board could be an ongoing exercise, with individuals continually adding things they want. This helps managers to actively engage in goal-orientated discussions.

The discussion could go something like this: 'Wesley, let's have a look at what you have in your pinboard. Which things have you added? OK you've added a car. Which car have you added? Have you test driven it yet? Is this the colour you want? When do you want the car by? Which do you want more, the holiday to the Maldives or the car?' It would go on from there. Done this way, it could encourage goal-orientated discussions to be a more regular feature of manager and sales consultant discussions.

Summary

The premise of this chapter is to show how the more aware a manager is of an individual's motivators, the easier it is to inspire higher levels of self-motivation. Often, individuals are not forthcoming in sharing their goals, so managers need to be consciously curious in asking what individuals want to achieve. Sometimes, employees are not consciously aware of what motivates them or they don't have solid goals they are looking to achieve. In these instances, the manager has a responsibility to help develop that individual's capability to understand their own motivators and to then create goals. Managers need to adapt their role from having a supervisory focus to having a coaching and development focus.

The aim of the exercises I included in this chapter is to provide a guide to what you can do to improve your team's awareness of their motivators and goals. There are countless other exercises that managers can run, but I think these serve as a good starting point. I hope you do too.

References

1 Sinek, S (2009) *Start with Why: How great leaders inspire everyone to take action*, Penguin
2 PWC (2011) *Millennials at Work: Reshaping the workplace* https://www.pwc.de/de/prozessoptimierung/assets/millennials-at-work-2011.pdf [last accessed 14/4/18]
3 Pink, D (2011) *Drive: The surprising truth about what motivates us*, Canongate Books
4 Goffee, R and Jones, G (2006) *Why Should Anyone Be Led By You? A guide to being an authentic leader*, Harvard Business Review Press

Prioritizing the alignment of company and employee goals

08

KEY CHAPTER TAKEAWAYS

- It's not good announcing a new strategy or change in direction and expecting employees to blindly follow and change.
- Managers need to connect the activities and behaviours required by their company with an individual's personal goals.
- Individual business plans can help increase alignment between company and individual goals.

Having spent many years in a corporate environment, as a sales consultant, a manager, director and internal trouble shooter, I can safely say that managers and directors rarely ask people to do something without there being a specific benefit for the company. Are people really excited enough about their work to run along and do their manager's bidding, just like that? Only engaged people will. In the UK, the 'engaged' cohort of employee accounts for just 17 per cent of the overall workforce, according to 2016 Gallup research. Engagement is better in the United States (32 per cent), but worse globally (15 per cent).[1]

A reason for this is employees often do not see a direct correlation between what they are asked to do and what they will gain personally for the benefit they will provide to others. Managers are not answering the question that almost every individual asks themselves when they are being asked to do things differently by their manager: 'What's in this for me?' It is not necessarily that managers do not care about whether someone gains personally from performing a requested activity; more often than not it is just that they assume that salary and bonuses are sufficient. Some assume that individuals will connect what is being asked of them with how they will gain personally.

Communicating company goals and aligning focus

Sometimes it can feel that your team is not as committed to the team's targets or goals as you are. But, how likely is it that your team will turn up every day and deliberately strive to stop you achieving the team target? I hope that, aside from the occasional individual, you feel that most people in your team come in to work to work hard and hit their targets. So where is the disconnect? The most common disconnect I find in companies is that individuals are just not aware of the goals, targets and plans of the team. You may have told them last week, but telling them does not necessarily mean they understand the goals and what is needed to achieve them.

This is an issue for many organizations as the process of communicating organizational goals and the strategy to achieve those goals is poorly executed and lacks transparency. However, organizations such as Intel, Google and Amazon manage to create a transparent framework where the organization can communicate its goals to all teams and employees. This is just the first step though. What happens next is that teams create their own strategies and goals to help the organization hit its own goals. This process then continues through the organization, the outcome being that individuals have clarity on the bigger goals of the organization and, more importantly, they have clarity on what their own role is and how it will be measured.

An approach created by Intel and made popular by John Doerr is called OKR (Objective and Key Results). The premise of this approach is that it allows every level of an organization to align their focus to the goals of the organization while allowing teams the freedom to decide on the best way for them to support the achievement of the wider organizational goals. This approach is now used by companies such as Google, Accenture, Adobe, Amazon and Anheuser-Busch.

The Objective aspect of OKR encourages a business to define clear goals for the organization or the team. Three to four key measurable results are then identified. These goals are meant to be 'stretch' goals, meaning that an objective is deemed completed when 70 per cent of the key results have been achieved. If 100 per cent of a key result is achieved, it is deemed not to have been stretching enough.

The 'best practice' approach is that every quarter (or defined period) a CEO will announce the OKRs of the organization and then each function, team and individual will create their own OKRs to align with the organization as a whole. In some companies all OKRs are visible across the organization and these OKRs then drive team and individual focus over the quarter. Finally, the OKRs form the basis for performance reviews.

I like the OKR approach for a number of reasons:

1 **Transparency**: This means individuals have clarity of what the organization is trying to achieve and the role their team has in achievement of this success.

2 **Dialogue**: It encourages a dialogue between teams, managers and employees as OKRs are created, which increases buy-in and engagement towards the goal.

3 **Stretch**: The ongoing focus on stretch goals creates an environment of continuous improvement. This can help sales teams move beyond a focus of just hitting targets.

4 **Data**: The focus on key measures allows organizations to measure the impact of changes.

As with all management approaches, there are other alternatives to OKR, for example *The 4 Disciplines of Execution* by Sean Covey.[2] I guess whatever approach you choose, the focus should be on spending time connecting what people are being asked to do with the contribution it makes to the team and the wider organization.

Does your team know your goals and plans?

So, to get you started, the first exercise in this chapter focuses on helping you understand whether your team is aware of the targets and goals and what the plans are to achieve those goals.

When it comes to assessing how well your team understands the strategic goals of the organization, you really need to get out of your chair and start talking to people. Many of you will have watched the TV show called *Undercover Boss*. In the show, business leaders go undercover in low level positions in their company to experience what it is really like to work for their business and what employees really think of those at the top. While I am not recommending you go undercover, it is always worthwhile taking the pulse of your organization from the view on the ground and raising your awareness about what your business thinks about your current strategy and how motivated they are to help you execute it.

There's a quick test I often advocate to leaders when asking them to investigate how aware their teams (marketing, sales, account managers and operations) are of team and company goals.

Quick test

Ask 10 people in your team or organization two simple questions:

1 What is the performance goal of the organization?
2 What is our current strategy to reach this goal?

All a manager has to then do is internally rate the quality of responses they get out of 10 (10 = excellent, 0 = very poor).

I love this simple test because leaders quickly establish whether their view that 'everyone is aware of the company's goals and what needs to be done' is true or false. From this simple exercise, you can soon work out what teams see as being their priorities and whether they are aligned with the organizational goals. Every person in your organization pointing in the wrong direction, even if it's only a slight misalignment, will increase the resistance facing your attempts to help the organization towards its collective goals. When you start investigating why individual or team priorities are not aligned, you may well find that it is not a deliberate choice, but the result of poor communication between the company, its executive and the wider management team.

The important caveat when doing this exercise is that if, when people do not know an organization's goals, the fault lies not with them, but with the organization's entire leadership team.

What's in it for me?

While we might be motivated by the goals of the organization, deep down when most people are asked to change what they are doing, they are thinking 'What's in this for me?' In fact, in many sales teams you do not have to go particularly deep to find a 'What's in this for me?' waiting to be spoken.

When I was trying to implement change as a sales manager, I was often frustrated by how quickly the 'What's in this for me?' statements arrived when I was suggesting change. However, as I reflect back on those conversations, I was probably a little blinkered in how I approached the conversations.

So, let's think about how you may handle this situation.

You've just left a meeting with your CEO or sales director, having just agreed to something that will involve lots of extra work. After this meeting you will typically have one of three feelings. You could feel excitement at the new opportunity you have been given. You could be happy yet sceptical that this is something that you want to do or frustrated that you are being made to do something that you do not want to do. To a large extent, how you feel is determined by whether you think the allotted task gives you want you want, as well as the company what they want.

An error many managers make is that they assume because someone has agreed to do something they have made the connection between what is being asked of them and what benefit they will get from completing a task or behaving in a certain way. I regularly ask individuals I spend time with as a trainer or coach 'Why does doing

<insert task / behaviour> help you be successful?' What never ceases to amaze me is the number of sales consultants or managers who say 'I do not know, I do it because my manager told me to do it this way.' While I admire their obedience, my concern is that their lack of understanding impacts their confidence and commitment to giving 100 per cent.

In a business as usual context this lack of understanding may well impact productivity levels when a manager's back is turned. In a situation where a team or organization is going through significant change a lack of understanding may lead to more disruptive behaviours. Imagine you have just been told by your manager you cannot do business with a client because the margins are too low. You may accept the decision, but if you did not understand why the decision would benefit you in the long run, what would you be feeling inside? What would you be saying to your colleagues at the water cooler?

While you may assume the person in your team will make the connection between what you are asking them to do and what they will get from doing it, the more proactive you are in helping them make that connection, the greater the chances are you will unlock higher levels of motivation. Like any good sales professional, managers need to be active in discussing both the positives and the negatives of a certain behaviour or activity. By acknowledging the potential downsides or anticipating potential concerns, the manager demonstrates that they understand what the person wants or is motivated by, even though what is being asked may not give the individual the desired outcome.

Manager tip: The sell back

An accepted sales technique is to ask a client that has just agreed to buy something to reiterate what benefits they feel they will get from XYZ product/service. This works as when a client verbalizes in their own words the reasons they have made a good decision, they reaffirm to themselves that they have made the right decision. However, it takes courage on the part of the sales professional; if the buyer has been pushed into a decision, they will struggle to articulate why they have bought and may begin to question why, which increases the likelihood of a cancellation.

The same approach can be used when someone in your team has just committed to do something differently. Stop and ask one more question: 'What benefit do you think you will get from changing <insert area of change>?'

This question is aimed at testing the level of understanding the individual has of how an agreed action will benefit them personally.

This question is difficult to ask as by asking it a manager raises the likelihood of exposing potential areas where the individual does not understand or accept what is being asked of them, meaning the manager has to reopen the conversation and resell the need to change and gain agreement to change. However, the upside is that the manager can address concerns rather than wait to observe evidence of non-agreement to surface in the following weeks.

Exercises to help you improve how you align company and individual goals

Back to basics

I remember two phrases from early on in my career that my managers repeated over and over again. Firstly, 'p**s poor planning causes p**s poor performance' and the second 'every conversation is a sales conversation'. Arguably, they are as relevant today as they were then. They are also relevant to any conversation you have where you are seeking to influence behaviour or activities. With this in mind, do you prepare for internal conversations as you would a client phone call or pitch meeting? The basics of sales technique need to be there: you need to build rapport, reclarify the person's needs, actively discuss topics where you know your client will have objections, deliver solutions as a set of pros and cons and not forgetting trial close along the way to ensure you are on the right track. It all needs to finish off with the client saying 'Can I do this please?' In essence, the quality of your conversation needs to make someone want to buy, rather than you having to follow a seven-step closing process or resort to saying 'Do it because I pay you to do it.'

Exercise

Preparing your meeting pitch

The next time you are about to have a meeting in which you need to ask someone to change their behaviour, ask yourself the following questions to prepare for the meeting and connect your sales brain with your manager brain:

Meeting preparation

i) Desired outcome

– What do I want this person to do after this meeting?

ii) Goals

– What is this person wanting to achieve professionally this year?

– What do they want to achieve personally?

– What do they already enjoy about their job?

iii) Issues

– Why might they not want to do what I am asking them to do?

– What other options do they have on the table?

– What has not gone their own way recently that may mean they are less willing to be flexible?

iv) Options

– What are possible solutions to this problem/situation?

– What are the pros and cons for the individual of each approach?

v) Commitment

– What are the different levels of commitment I am willing to accept?

Goal comparison

People approach their sales budgets for the following year in different ways. Some build budgets from the ground up, working out what sales are already agreed and what each individual and team is good to deliver on. Then they add the individual numbers together to create a team number, followed by adding teams to teams to create divisional targets etc. Others just take last year's figures, add 20, 30 or 40 per cent and then begin the process of sharing the sales targets between each division, then with teams and then down to individuals. However you approach it, at the end of the process each person and team will have a number on their head. The danger for sales managers is that if there is a disconnect between the company goal and the goals of the individual and challenging times hit, the likelihood of the sales consultant going the extra mile to hit the target is diminished. Why? Because that person's perception of who owns the target will impact their commitment to doing whatever it takes to achieve it.

My personal view is that individuals typically see 'targets' as owned by a company, where 'goals' are more likely to be perceived as owned by individuals. This means the skill of a great sales manager is being able to take the budget target and work with individuals to align their personal goals with the goals of the company. This next exercise is intended to help managers have an open dialogue with individuals and teams to help them align their targets and goals. A prerequisite of this exercise is that everyone will need some sort of target assigned to them or have created their own personal goals.

Exercise

Goal comparison and discussion

Once a manager has allocated sales budgets to each person in their team, they can have a goal comparison discussion with each person in their team. This discussion involves no more than the manager asking someone in their team what their fee or sales goal is for the coming year and comparing the two numbers.

Ideally there will be similarity between the two numbers, which means the conversation can move on to what the manager can do to support the sales consultant achieve their goals. Where there is a mismatch the manager and sales consultant can discuss the reason for it. When the sales consultant has a number significantly larger than the manager's, the manager may ask:

- How did you come up with that number?
- This will mean you need to grow X% or £XXX next year; how will you achieve that growth?

Where appropriate they may encourage a more realistic number.

If the manager's budgeted number is larger than the sales consultant's they may ask:

- Why was your number so low?

- What do you think of the number I have budgeted for you?

- What would stop you reaching that number?

- What number would be more realistic?

- What extra support could we provide to help you feel you can achieve more?

Ultimately you will know what questions are most relevant for your team.

The purpose of this exercise is to encourage managers to engage their teams in goals and budgets before the year starts. This way expectations are aligned before the year starts and the pressure to deliver arrives.

Business planning

Whether individuals are working to achieve a target you have set or a goal they are striving towards, everyone needs a plan. The challenge is that in the early days in a person's career, they may need a structured operating model to work from. Those sales consultants further down their career path want more flexibility to create a plan that matches their own needs. I remember very clearly sitting with a manager and objecting to being asked the same questions, week after week, even though I had 18 months of experience. The response from my manager was 'Go away, make your own plan up. I will be your investor. Each week we will review your plan. If I do not think it is good or you are not executing it, I will withdraw funding...' You might think my motivation was impacted by the implication that 'funding being withdrawn' implied getting fired; however, my response was higher levels of motivation to plan my own success.

How much of my plan was the company's standard plan? The answer is quite a lot. Was the conversation any different? No. We still talked about leads, client meetings, placements made etc. The difference was that I felt like I was in control of how I went about hitting my own goals.

So, how much freedom do you give to your experienced sales professionals to create their own business plan that they can follow to hit their goals? It may be that you cannot give flexibility on the target each person has; however, helping them create a plan that they own can increase levels of ownership. Think about how the OKR approach helps individuals in companies such as Intel, Google or Amazon feel like they have a greater say in how their performance will be measured. This can also apply to the planning around sales targets.

The challenge for managers is that it is easy enough to hand over a success template. Much harder is to train and coach someone to produce a plan that is sufficiently detailed to succeed. It takes time and effort. However, the upside is that by teaching someone to create their own plan, you are increasing the likelihood of their performance being self-sustaining. As the old adage says 'give a man a fish and you feed him for a day; teach a man to fish, and you feed him for a lifetime'.

What you include in the business plan is up to you, but the most effective plans I see focus, not on the numbers that will be achieved, but on the operational plan to achieve the goals. The component parts will be different, according to the make-up of your sales role, but a typical sales consultant will have a plan for a) network nurturing and lead generation, b) lead conversion and c) client retention and expansion. The aim of this process is that when a sales professional builds their own plan, they will have a greater level of ownership of the plan and are therefore more likely to execute it than if they were following an inflexible template given to them by their manager.

This is an example plan for a B2B sales consultant:

Part 1: Goals and purpose

Earnings:

- What do I want to earn?
- Why do I want to earn this?

Billings:

- What do I want to bill to meet my earnings target?
- What am I billing at the moment?
- By how much do I need to increase my billings?

Goals:

- What do I want to achieve this year personally?
- What do I want to achieve professionally?

Part 2: Network nurture and lead generation

Improving sales process:

- Sourcing of new prospects and initiating contact.
- Nurturing of existing qualified prospects.
- Organization of target lists.

Learning:

- What skills do I need to learn or improve?

Measures:

- Key metrics (volume or effectiveness).

Part 3: Lead conversion

Improving sales process:

- Qualification and prioritization of leads.
- Lead nurturing and conversation.

Learning:

- What skills do I need to learn or improve?

Measures:

- Key metrics (volume or effectiveness).

Part 4: Client retention and expansion

Improving sales process:

- Gaining feedback on service delivery.
- Adding value to existing clients to maintain front of mind awareness.
- Increasing range of services and growing revenues in key accounts.

Learning:

- What skills do I need to learn or improve?

Measures:

- Key metrics (volume or effectiveness).

This is a very rough outline of a business plan that a sales consultant could produce. You will undoubtedly be able to create a business plan outline that more closely matches your own business. The key to success is that it is focused on WHAT an individual is going to do to hit their target and HOW they are going to do things differently than last year.

Summary

In summary, while the previous chapter focused on learning about the goals and aspirations of your team, this chapter focused on helping you, as a manager, to connect the team or organizational goals to the goals and aspirations of your team. The key point is that alignment is a lot more than an element of the annual appraisal process. It is the day-to-day dialogue between you and your team.

References

1 Mann, A and Harter, J (2016) *The Worldwide Employee Engagement Crisis* http://news.gallup.com/businessjournal/188033/worldwide-employee-engagement-crisis.aspx [last accessed 14/4/18]

2 Covey, S (2012) *The 4 Disciplines of Execution: Achieving your wildly important goals*, Simon & Schuster

Avoid the smart 09 dumb paradox

Your team is a gold mine of ideas

KEY CHAPTER TAKEAWAYS

- The smart dumb paradox: companies hire smart people, but too often treat them as if they are dumb.
- Leaders should be interested in what their teams have to say.
- Acknowledgement of issues increases engagement.

You don't have to be smart to be successful in sales in today's market but it certainly helps. Neil Rackham, author, consultant and academic, who is an expert on consultative selling, pointed out a number of years ago that millions of sales jobs would disappear and the era of getting well paid for taking orders would soon be over.[1]

This is taken a step further in the book *The Challenger Sale* (2013),[2] written by Matthew Dixon and Brent Adamson, managing directors of the sales executive council at the best practice insights and technology company, CEB. In this book, sales reps are told that just building relationships with customers is not enough. You don't talk to customers about facts and figures, but challenge them and educate them by giving them insights about how they could achieve their goals.

However, there is a paradox (isn't there always?!) and it's this: on one hand, sales teams need to be smarter, but on the other, leadership teams often still treat their sales teams as if they are dumb. This is the smart dumb paradox. Let me explain...

When it comes to implementing change, management often treat their teams as if they are anything but smart. Let's look at what happens when the sales team are behaving smartly, but management is treating them as if they are dumb. So, you have a smart sales team working hard at nurturing relationships and generating leads. They are adapting their approach based on evolving client demands and fast-changing buying processes. They are also constantly adapting their approach to counter what their competitors are up to. While all of this is going on, they are hitting or, ideally, exceeding their targets. Then there is a catalyst for change (eg economic environment, falling sales pipeline, new competitor etc), prompting the executive team to come up with a change of strategy. At some point, everyone is gathered together in a room and the 'new strategy' or 'focus area' is announced. Cue the normal range of emotions you would expect from a sales team. So far, this all sounds predictably normal.

What makes this approach dumb is that those leadership teams are approaching this process the same way they did 50 years ago. Even though times have changed and changed a lot. They are assuming that the sales team has nothing useful to say or contribute to the strategy. Their opinion is often not considered. It so often happens that the executive team formulates a new change strategy, with either very little or no prior consultation with those who have to implement the strategy. Not only that – those who have to implement the strategy arguably have a clearer insight into why a change of strategy might be required and why clients are choosing competitors because these are the people talking to existing, past and potential clients day in, day out.

An example of the smart dumb paradox in day-to-day sales operations would be how companies use sales KPIs. It is common for companies to have a standard set of KPIs, which sales teams are measured by. In some instances, these KPIs are adapted to meet the individual circumstances of each team. However, in the main, they are not adapted to the different demands of different market segments. At some point, though, there will be a 'push' on one particular metric. For example, people will be told 'This quarter, we need to focus on more client meetings, demos or sales calls.' This is pushed hard across all teams, even those where that particular metric is not relevant or achievable, based on how a particular market segment works. That is what I call the dumb approach. It doesn't work very well. What would be the smart way of driving change? It would be to ask each team to pick one metric that they could improve that would help them hit their sales targets, which is how the OKR approach works. However, from a senior leadership perspective, this approach lacks clarity and the ability to directly compare teams and feel they are focusing on the right thing.

To be fair, this approach worked pretty well for 50 years, largely, because senior leadership teams often did know more about what strategies worked best in certain situations. The pace of market change was a lot slower then, so when a new approach was needed, leaders could draw on their own experience as a sales professional or on the organizational playbook for what action should be taken when.

There are two reasons why this approach doesn't work so well anymore. Firstly, most sales professionals existed in a type of 'knowledge poverty' in the past. Their awareness of what competitors were doing and charging and what products customers were buying was limited to what they experienced in their roles, so when change was announced, sales consultants were hungry for the advice on what to do to overcome business or market challenges. In today's world, there is an abundance of knowledge. Individuals have access to the same knowledge as their leaders and they are smart – they will have their own view on what change is needed. Arguably, in many instances the salespeople on the ground have a greater level of knowledge than their leadership.

The second reason a top-down approach to change works less well is, of course, the current speed of change. Many leaders are now running teams where they have no experience of selling in that market and, more importantly, executing a sales process that is outside their comfort zone. By this I am referring to the prevalence of tech-enabled communications, such as communication platforms, email and social media. These have become an essential part of the sales process (and an essential part of working life) and they are now just as important as phone calls and face-to-face meetings. Yet I regularly meet leaders who bemoan tools such as email and social media, calling them a distraction from 'true' business development.

The challenge for leaders is that the consequences of the paradox are not immediately evident. This is because the effects are more like sandpaper against the skin than being hit with a hammer. Imagine how you would feel if you were continually being asked to do things that you felt were not tailored to your market or that you knew were the wrong thing to do based on your own market knowledge. While everyone can accept their leaders making the odd bad call, when they keep happening it erodes the individual's belief in their leader. More specifically, it erodes the belief that the leadership team has the capability to guide the organization successfully through market challenges to achieve its stated aims.

There are two main indicators that tell me that the smart dumb paradox exists in an organization. Firstly, I see a regular flow of experienced talent leave the business; this tends to be sales consultants who can operate independently when building and leveraging a client base. They are the individuals who are most affected when they see the leadership team making what they perceive to be the wrong decisions and not engaging them in the creation of plans. Secondly, there is an underlying scepticism about the leadership team's willingness to listen to the challenges that sales, marketing and operations teams are experiencing. Comments you often hear are 'That's just the way the system works' and 'There's no point telling them because they will not change it.'

Now this does not mean that a senior leadership team cannot or should not make unpopular decisions. What I am saying is that the more widely they engage people in the organization with thinking about and discussing current challenges and the potential solutions, the more understanding, acceptance and tolerance will be present when changes are made.

I have to hold my hand up here though and make an admission. I have been victim to the smart dumb paradox. Over my career I have been responsible for implementing strategies that have come from far off lands, even though they were not always right for the market I worked in. I have helped create strategies that worked to reinforce what the leadership team thought was the right way of doing things. I have done what I have just told you not do to: I have treated smart people as if they were dumb. In any sales environment where market conditions are changing quickly or where there is a high level of competition, it is incredibly difficult to not become victim to the smart dumb paradox. Decisions need to be made, often quickly, and often there is not actually a right choice. You make what you hope is the best choice, given time and knowledge constraints.

I hope that the exercises and examples given in this chapter help leaders engage with their teams more frequently, helping them to create the right strategy and, ultimately, have teams that are more motivated to execute change.

When starting the process of treating your sales teams like the smart people that they are, it is important that you are clear in your own mind and the minds of your wider leadership team what you are trying to achieve. If you are only just starting out down the 'smart route', there will be a certain level of scepticism about your true intentions and whether your desire to engage is a fad or a lasting change in approach. Possible goals could be:

Approach 1: Are you interested in what they have to say?

Your team members need to feel that you are genuinely interested in what they have to say. Think about it from the perspective of a service engineer, for example. They are on client sites every day, seeing how they use the product or service and helping them through the challenges they have in using the company's products onsite. Every day they are dealing first-hand with the quirks of your product or service and they see the impact these issues have on customer satisfaction and retention. Equally, every day sales teams will be learning about what services your competitors are offering and what they are charging for their services. They will be learning how companies are looking to insource services that were previously outsourced, such as marketing, procurement, recruiting and finance. This internal and external market insight is critical for the senior leadership to hear if they want to understand whether or not their service offering meets the needs of the customers.

What the leadership needs to ensure is that there is a mechanism for everyone in the organization to feedback, not just the limitations of the product or service, but also market insights that will affect the long-term success of the organization.

Concept applied

Elon Musk, founder of Tesla, demonstrated an openness with his approach to communication across Tesla. His belief is communication through a traditional approach where ideas, challenges and suggestions move within the chain of command is inefficient and 'dumb'.

He believes that:

Anyone at Tesla can and should email/talk to anyone else according to what they think is the fastest way to solve a problem for the benefit of the whole company. You can talk to your manager's manager without his permission, you can talk directly to a VP in another dept, you can talk to me, you can talk to anyone without anyone else's permission. Moreover, you should consider yourself obligated to do so until the right thing happens. The point here is not random chitchat, but rather ensuring that we execute ultra-fast and well. We obviously cannot compete with the big car companies in size, so we must do so with intelligence and agility.[3]

This extract was taken from an email that Elon Musk sent to Tesla employees.

Approach 2: Acknowledge awareness of the issues

The second message individuals want to believe is that their concerns have been heard. When communicating changes, instructions and operational plans, it's important to reference the catalyst for these changes. Sometimes leaders think that their employees will naturally make that connection, but they often don't. When a leader says 'This is what we have heard and this is what we're doing to address this problem or meet the market need...' individuals are more likely to feel confident that the issues affecting the company's ability to grow are being heard and acted upon. This then increases the likelihood of engagement of employees' discretionary effort.

Approach 3: Authenticity around why decisions are made

Organizations tend to be a lot better at highlighting what needs to be done than they are at articulating why decisions are being made or why actions have been taken. The challenge managers face is how to deliver the rationale behind change. Managers are often nervous of sharing the true reason for a decision being made, especially if it relates to the company struggling financially. However, Phil Jones, CEO of Brother UK, recently said to me 'People's ability to handle the truth is greater than we perceive.' When communicating news, managers need to be credible and not just perceived as repeating the corporate message. When individuals feel that the rationale behind change is corporate speak, there is a lower level of motivation to change. In these instances, cynics tend to actively look for the subtext of any message or change. When leaders articulate change, they and all the other tiers of management need to be willing and able to explain why the change is happening and the options that were considered before this particular decision was made.

As with everything in sales and marketing, your chances of success are greatly improved if you think about how you want your prospect to feel after your email, phone call or meeting. The same is true for internal engagement. Start this process by thinking about how you want your team to think differently and about your willingness to engage them in the creation of your sales and marketing strategy.

Approach 4: Change is like building a car

One of the reasons sales processes are becoming more complex is that buying managers have a greater aversion to risk. No one wants to be responsible for buying a product or service that does not work out. As a result, instead of making decisions based on their own judgement, as managers used to do, they now seek a far wider range of opinions on whether buying a product or service is a good thing. Why do they do this? Because the more fingerprints there are attached to a buying decision, the less likely it is that one person will be held accountable if things go wrong.

I take a similar approach when working with executive teams, but for a different reason. I do it because I believe that the more people that are involved in creating a strategy, the greater the likelihood is of it being owned by everyone and implemented effectively. The challenge from an executive team's perspective is how to give everyone a say and still feel confident that the strategy is what the business needs, because when there are lots of conflicting views, experience levels and advice, it can be hard to reach a consensus. The answer is to treat organizational change like building a car.

At a simple level, there are three parts to building a car:

Part one: Setting the parameters of the car and what market segment it is targeted at. This is things like size, price point, efficiency and the number of units to be sold. In essence, the executive team would dictate the chassis of the car and the parameters that the car will be built around.

Part two: The car designers are given the parameters. They design the car that they think meets the needs of the company and the needs of the customers.

Part three: The customer gets the chance to adapt the car so that they feel they are getting exactly what they want. This involves them choosing the colour, engine, trim level, wheels and, lastly, personalized items such as fluffy dice!

The ideal situation is that everyone is happy. The executives are happy because they built a car that hit a certain market segment and they sold the number of units needed. Whether or not they liked the car they built or liked what customers did with that car is irrelevant to them. The car designers are happy because they had the freedom to build the car they wanted to build. They saw customers buy their car and they will hopefully sell more than the competition. In all likelihood, they care little about whether or not fluffy dice now swing freely from the internal mirror (although, that said, some designers will care a great deal!). The customer is happy because they got the car they wanted and were able to make it unique to them. Win, Win, Win.

This approach can also be applied to implementing change in sales teams.

Concept applied

Overview: Management Consultancy t/o 30m, circa 100 consultants.

Challenge: Only the managing partners were directly responsible for the sales pipeline. There were challenges with getting the extended leadership team engaged with proactively generating and nurturing future opportunities. The wider consultant group had little awareness of their ability to find potential opportunities for new business while on clients' sites. Lastly Salesforce had been implemented but was rarely used to track the sales pipeline.

Action

Meeting 1: Building the chassis

Managing partner and two senior partners spend half a day defining what they need from the sales process, such as:

- visibility of future opportunities' value;
- value of opportunities at pitch stage and forecast of what will close this month;
- the use of Salesforce;
- revenue, gross margin and margin percentage targets.

Meeting 2: Designing the car

All managing partners in a half-day session. Focused on:

- defining the customer buying journey;
- defining a sales process to match the buying journey;
- defining how salesforce should be used;
- metrics and ratios that will measure activity within pipeline;
- managing partners defining areas of the process where they have a strength and would want to be involved in developing the process further (not everyone feels comfortable pitching for business just as some loathe writing proposals).

Meeting 3: Pimping the ride

All consultants and leadership in a two-hour workshop style session. The 40-minute workshops cover:

- The customer buying journey, understanding the customer journey, allowing consultants to make improvements.

- The sales process, understanding awareness of each stage.

- A demonstration of how using Salesforce can help support the sales process and nurturing client relationships.

- Individuals were able to suggest areas where they would add value to the sales process or indicate areas where they wanted to be involved but needed more training.

After the third meeting there was significantly more awareness and buy-in to the sales process. Importantly in an environment typically averse to 'sales' talk, there was more acceptance and appreciation of how 'sales' activity can be performed but not conflict with the values of being a management consultant.

This works because by the end of the process everyone has had a chance to influence what the strategy will be in order to achieve the revenue and profit goals of the organization. It works on another level in that if targets are missed, it gives each party (executive, leadership and sales consultants) a chance to investigate where the plan worked and where it failed. They can then engage in discussions about how the plan will be different next time.

What happens if you do not want to build a car?

If you like the idea of everyone being part of building the plan but do not want to build a car, then I encourage you to flick back to the previous chapter where I highlight how companies such as Intel, Google, Amazon and more use the OKR approach to goal setting. Whether you choose OKR or the building a car approach, the goal is that every team and person gets the freedom to set their own objectives and measures to help the organization hit its own goals (financial and operational).

Next time you need to change your sales strategy, if you are a CEO or sales director, set your parameters, give objectives and measures to your leadership team to design the broader plan, then help them engage the sales team in designing the details of the plan and how each of these details will be measured. The most important part of this is the sales team defining how they want to be held accountable for the execution of their plan.

Approach 5: How do you solve a problem like...

In 2006, there was a reality talent show in the UK called *How Do You Solve A Problem Like Maria*? The aim of the show was to find a previously undiscovered actress to play the part of Maria in a new stage show of *The Sound of Music*. The title inferred that the audience had a part to play in finding the ideal Maria. Since then, I have run many, many workshops where I have borrowed the premise of the title. I hope that you will too after reading this part of the chapter.

A great way to start a positive and proactive discussion with your leadership or sales team is to pose a problem that you need to solve. This works for both parties concerned because it allows leadership to set the parameters of the problem to be solved, while at the same time giving an open invite for sales professionals to engage in finding a solution.

Here's a simple exercise that requires little more explanation than following a simple five-step process to facilitate a discussion that takes your team from problem to agreed action plan:

Step 1: Outline the problem that needs to be solved.

Step 2: Agree what the ideal should be or what things would look like if the problem was solved.

Step 3: Discuss the reasons this problem occurs and why previous attempts to solve the problem have failed.

Step 4: Consider options available to solve this issue (focus discussion on realistic changes that the team can control or influence).

Step 5: Agree an action plan with the team that leaves both manager and sales consultants with actions to execute.

The 'How do we solve a problem like…' approach can be used in a number of different situations.

1 Strategy

Long-term plan to win: in most organizations, everybody is aware of how technology or process re-engineering is impacting how people buy their category of product or service. Most will have seen companies such as Yell and Kodak disappear, all because the organizations did not adapt or change quickly enough to the market situation. Leaders need to be able to communicate what their organization's place will be in the future marketplace. However, it may be that sales, marketing or operations teams will have suggestions that can help the executive team. This will then give the executive or leadership team the platform to gather opinion on their thoughts on future market strategy.

Discussion starter question

How do we solve the problem of our customers expecting more service for a lower price?

---

2 Financial awareness

Sometimes leaders need to make decisions based on what the numbers show, rather than how they feel. Such decisions are not usually popular. However, I find that where teams have a higher level of financial understanding, they are more able to rationalize the changes being made, even if they do not agree with them. For instance, you hear that the bonus pool is being cut; naturally, you would be unhappy about this. However, how would your view change if your manager sat down and talked through the profit and loss statement and discussed the other options they had considered before making this decision? It might be that you think of other potential cost savings, which are better than cutting the bonus pool option. By increasing managers' and sales teams' general awareness and appreciation of organizational finance, you help them to understand the difficult decisions that need to be made.

Discussion starter question

How do we save £XYZ per year? <or insert another financial stat to suit>

CASE STUDY   Media agency

An example of this in action came from a friend during the recession in 2009. He ran a marketing agency that had been affected by the banking crisis. He was reluctant to make redundancies so focused his cost-saving efforts on reducing the costs of running the business. Pretty soon he had to start making decisions like should they keep the free coffee, would there be a Christmas party etc. There were no easy choices left. In a moment of enlightenment he called a meeting of all 25 staff and laid out the situation. He put out on the table about 20 cards, each with an area of discretionary spend written on it and the cost associated with that activity.

He posed a challenge to the team, saying 'We needed to save £X thousand pounds. Some of these things we can stop doing, others we can reduce and others we can keep. You need to work together to decide what we do with each one.'

After 90 minutes the team had decided they wanted a smaller Christmas party, and cake and presents on birthdays would stop but critically the free filtered coffee would stay.

Was everyone happy? NO. But did people feel better they had had a say? YES.

---

3 Operational efficiency

In most organizations, the people fulfilling a function on the ground are best placed to know about the inefficiencies that exist within the organization. Leadership and the executive team will gain a far better understanding of the problems they are facing and potential solutions by engaging in open discussions with those experiencing the effects and inefficiencies day to day.

> ## Discussion starter question
>
> How do we solve our <insert operational efficiency issue> problem?

4 Systems

Sales, marketing and operations teams have a troubled relationship with their internal CRM. The CRM is often built to service such a broad range of interest groups that it doesn't give anyone what they want. As a result, individuals see the system as an inhibitor of success, rather than enabler. Hitting people with a data entry stick does not work. In fact, it is more likely to perpetuate the belief that you do not understand what it takes to be successful in today's market. A more consultative sales approach is needed to engage sales and marketing teams in using the CRM more productively.

> ## Discussion starter question
>
> How do we solve the problem of missed opportunities because of poor data quality in the CRM?

CASE STUDY CRM usage

Company: US $250m t/o European subsidiary of global IT company

Situation: EMEA soon to implement Salesforce but poor adoption after US roll-out meant the software had a terrible internal reputation. EMEA sales consultants were nervous and moving back to spreadsheets.

Solution: The US organization's approach had been to mandate usage but the EMEA VP of sales decided to take a different approach. He sat his whole sales organization in a conference centre and asked them to define what information they would need out of Salesforce to make the effort of data input worthwhile.

Action: Post meeting he invested in the creation of sales dashboards to help the sales team manage leads, pitch processes and identify client expansion opportunities. Importantly some of these dashboards were customer facing which helped the sales professional in service review meetings.

Result: The EMEA Region had the highest usage of Salesforce globally and achieved quarter-on-quarter growth ahead of the company average.

5 Preparing for bad news

Another way to use this approach is to engage teams in open discussion when bad news is announced. Doing this allows open sharing of frustrations, anger or other demotivating emotions in an open forum. The intention of the discussion is that once the frustrations have been shared, the discussion can move on to how the impact of these changes can be minimized, both on an organizational and individual level. For example, in 2017 the UK rail company Great Western Railway electrified its trains. The transition from diesel to electric meant that the engineering and maintenance teams were significantly impacted. Train maintenance was moved from its traditional location and conducted by the train's manufacturer. This had the potential to significantly impact the motivation levels of the whole organization. In preparation for this change, the executive team arranged a leadership conference, which focused on helping leaders be more comfortable with discussing the upcoming changes and linking it to the long history of change and innovation in the railways.

Discussion starter question

<insert event> is about to happen. How do we overcome its impact on our team's motivation levels?

---

6 Connection of global to local

In a world where corporations are globally dispersed, it is increasingly hard for organizations to apply a corporate strategy across multiple markets and locations. Corporate head office may only see differences between countries and markets as nuances in approach and thus, too insignificant to worry about. However, from the perspective of those individuals working in those different markets, the nuances are an important part of how they promote and sell their service.

Think about a situation where you have a parent company whose main market supports high margins, yet the local subsidiary works in a market that is at a more advanced stage of commoditization. The local subsidiary will have higher degrees of pricing pressure and a broader range of competition. The corporate head office will be asking for high margins and growth and will base their expectations upon their understanding of their own market, rather than the local market. In many instances this can leave the local sales teams feeling frustrated that the HQ does not understand their specific market. It could be they are demotivated by being targeted or focused on sales outcomes that are significantly harder to achieve than in other markets.

The art of engaging discretionary effort is important here. The head office needs to be clear on what they want the outcome to be, but flexible about how the local management team craft the best strategy to deal with specific market challenges. The most effective description I have heard of this process is 'Think of it like a piece of music: we play the same tune as everyone else, just in a key and tempo that appeals to our local market.'

Discussion starter question

This is what HQ wants us to do. <insert HQ message/strategy> How do we make this strategy work for our market?

Summary

If you want higher levels of commitment to executing sales strategy, then you need to give a wide range of people the chance to contribute to the formulation of the strategy. The speed of marketplace change, and the availability of knowledge mean that treating your sales, marketing and operational teams as if they are dumb will affect, not just the execution of your plan, but also the quality of the plan itself. The more people you have contributing to the strategy, the greater the likelihood that there will be buy-in to executing the change. A great audiobook that covers this in more detail is *The 4 Disciplines of Execution: Achieving your wildly important goals*, by Chris McChesney and Sean Covey (2014).[4]

References

1 Rackham, N (2014) *Rackham on Sales* https://www.youtube.com/watch?v=KTRvRTqGNA4 Speakers.com [last accessed 14/4/18]

2 Dixon, M and Adamson, B (2013) *The Challenger Sale: How to take control of the customer conversation*, Portfolio Penguin

3 Bariso, J (2017) *This Email from Elon Musk to Tesla Employees Describes What Great Communication Looks Like*, Inc.com https://www.inc.com/justin-bariso/this-email-from-elon-musk-to-tesla-employees-descr.html [last accessed 14/4/18]

4 McChesney, C and Covey, S (2014) *The 4 Disciplines of Execution: Achieving your wildly important goals*, Franklin Covey

PART FOUR
Creating a mutually productive work environment

Have you ever been in a situation where you agreed to do something, then while doing it you realized that you had opened a can of worms? Well, when it comes to organizational values, it is a big can of worms. If I covered this topic properly, I could easily fill another book or three.

Values are easy things to write and post on your intranet and website, but they are far harder to execute in reality. In many organizations, the sales team operates under a different set of values to everyone else in the organization. I say this not so much from the perspective of the sales teams, but from the perspective of the rest of the organization. Professionals from other departments often say that sales teams view the world through a different lens.

Test this assumption out. Talk to a few people in finance, HR, IT or operations and ask them 'What do you think the values of the sales teams are?' You will hear all you need to know about how your sales team is viewed. Probably the best quote I have heard over the years was from a hard-pressed credit controller who summed up how many saw their sales team:

> Their values revolve around me, myself and I. If they are not going to get paid extra for doing something extra, then they make a song and dance about doing it. They are the rainmaker so surely we should all bow before them...

Pretty damning stuff. While this may not be the case in your organization, it has been the default in many businesses for many years.

I should also add that sales teams are not the only professionals to come in for this kind of criticism. I have friends working in law and accounting firms who say that some partners assume prophet-like status because of their ability to win business but are reluctant to introduce other partners to their clients.

To some extent the status quo between 'rainmaker' and everyone else in the organization has worked for the last 60 or 70 years. However, testing times are challenging this philosophy. As previously outlined, evolving buyer behaviour and alternative service providers mean that sales, marketing and delivery processes are increasingly intertwined. This means that values need to be more intertwined. Whereas it used to be possible for the sales team to have a different set of values to the rest of the organization, that kind of set-up no longer works. Disparities between the sales team's established values and the values of the wider organization can create friction between different teams. At worst, departments can end up actively working to undermine each other.

As we look to define what core values are key to a successful business development culture, I should probably clarify what I mean by core values.

Here's a pretty good description:

> **Core values** are the fundamental beliefs of the organization. They define how the company and its employees go about their work in serving equally the interests of customers, colleagues and the company. Core values are the guiding principles that dictate behaviour and help every employee understand the difference between right and wrong. Upholding an organization's core values is a condition of service not conditional on payment of additional bonuses or incentives.[1]

If you need an example of the potential consequences of a sales culture that has lost its way, you need look no further than the global financial crisis of 2008. There are countless stories of the desire for sales success being achieved not only at the expense of the customer, but also the organization as a whole. In the aftermath of the financial crisis, a whole raft of regulatory frameworks have been introduced. One of the most interesting changes within the banking industry has been the creation of the Banking Standards Board (BSB) in 2015. Interestingly, the BSB was created by the industry itself to 'promote high standards of behaviour and competence across UK banks and building societies'.[2]

While a cynic would be justified in thinking this is just another industry body that will serve the banks' interests before everyone else's, the board has approached matters in a slightly different way. Rather than being a trade body, the goal is to 'provide challenge, support and scrutiny for firms committed to rebuilding the sector's reputation, and it will provide impartial and objective assessments of the industry's progress', according to Sir Brendan Barber,[3] deputy chairperson at the BSB. It is the assessment part that interests me most. While they assume individually banks will have their own

Figure P4.1 BSB assessment framework

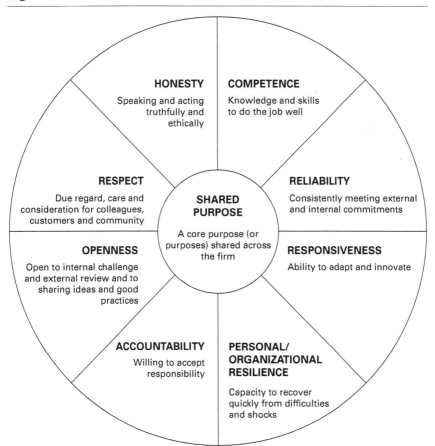

set of values, their framework is predicated on 'characteristics' that they associate with a bank or building society having a good culture. The BSB characteristics aim to ensure that banks and building societies focus on serving the needs of customers, employees and broader society. The 'characteristics' cover areas such as shared purpose, honesty, respect, reliability, responsiveness, accountability, resilience, openness, and competence.[4]

What stands out is that the banks submit themselves to both qualitative and quantitative assessments on an annual basis. The quantitative process is an independently run BSB Employee Survey sent to 106,000 employees in 2017 (82,000 employees in 2016); receiving more than 36,000 responses (28,000 responses in 2016) from across 25 participating banks and building societies in 2017 (22 in 2016). The assessment survey questions directly probe into the adherence of the whole company to the characteristics in the BSB Assessment Framework it has signed up to. I have listed a few of the sample questions below. The qualitative research involves the BSB running discussion groups across all levels of an organization, providing a deep understanding of how a firm is performing.

BSB assessment questions

These are some of the questions the BSB use in their assessments:

HONESTY
Q1: I believe senior leaders in my organization mean what they say.
Q2: In my organization I see instances where unethical behaviour is rewarded.

RESPECT
Q5: At my work I feel that I am treated with respect.
Q9: I believe my organization puts customers at the centre of business decisions.

OPENNESS
Q11: In my organization, people are encouraged to provide customers with information in a way that helps them make the right decisions.
Q14: If I raised concerns about the way we work, I would be worried about the negative consequences for me.

ACCOUNTABILITY
Q17: I see people in my organization turn a blind eye to inappropriate behaviour.
Q19: I feel comfortable challenging a decision made by my manager.

RESILIENCE
Q27: My organization focuses primarily on short-term results.

RESPONSIVENESS
Q30: I believe that my organization responds effectively to staff feedback.
Q34: I have observed improvements in the way we do things based on lessons learnt.

SHARED PURPOSE
Q36: There is no conflict between my organization's stated values and how we do business.

FREE TEXT QUESTION
Q37: What 3 words would you use to describe your organization?

What is interesting as you read through the full set of questions is that you can attribute almost every question to the banking industry's cultural failure in the run-up to the financial crisis. The 'characteristics' that have been created are targeted at changing those behaviours that contributed to past failures. Every person in the member firm gets to rate their organization's adherence to their professed 'characteristics' every year. This potentially makes it a very powerful tool to drive behavioural change.

You need to ask yourself what would happen if you created a similar set of questions to assess how well your company lives its values. How well would the whole company do and how well would your sales team rank?

And I guess this is the point of this section of the book. As more people in the organization have a role in the sales process, it is no longer feasible for the sales team to operate with a different set of values to everyone else. This is from both a wider employee motivation perspective and the efficient running of a business.

The three core values I will focus on for this section of the book are collaboration, confidence and capability, and performance expectation.

I think these three values are critically important and you will find out why as you read on.

References

1 Your dictionary http://examples.yourdictionary.com/examples-of-core-values.html#FFVGw1xx2vuUE4mo.99, [last accessed 14/4/18]

2 Banking Standards Board, What is the BSB? https://www.bankingstandardsboard.org.uk/what-is-the-bsb/ [last accessed 14/4/18]

3 https://www.bankingstandardsboard.org.uk/deputychairmanappointed/

4 Permission to share the BSB's 'characteristic' image and assessment questions kindly granted by the Banking Standards Board (www.bankingstandardsboard.org)

Why collaboration 10 is key to integrating sales culture

KEY CHAPTER TAKEAWAYS

- Collaboration is one of the most important values for companies looking to create a strong, effective business development environment.
- Collaboration is a key skill in today's workplace.
- Discussions that managers can have to improve collaboration within teams.

Humans are an organization's greatest asset and their greatest liability. Humans working together can achieve more than just one person. As the ancient Greek philosopher, Aristotle, said 'The whole is greater than the sum of its parts.' However, humans can also directly contribute to organizational inefficiency and the delivery of a variable product or customer experience.

Sales teams have historically been able to resist many process and technology changes as success has typically been defined by whether targets were hit and because compensations schemes focus on individual efforts. In many cases, companies tolerate behaviour from their sales consultants that in other departments would result in the termination of employment. Imagine what would happen if a member of the finance team or customer services refused to use the finance or CRM system, preferring instead to use their own spreadsheets.

But times are changing and there are five key reasons why collaboration between the sales teams and the wider organization is increasingly important:

1: The sales process

Changing buyer behaviour is forcing marketing and sales to become a single integrated process, rather than the traditional process of 'you get them in the room and I will close them'.

2: Knowledge is data

While all sales, marketing and operations teams rely on data to help with their decision making, the difference with tech companies is that they connect the data across their functions and the wider Internet to enable them to better market services and convert needs into revenues. Traditional companies need to better leverage their data across functions to aid a unified approach to business development.

3: Lead generation

As the world becomes increasingly networked, the chances are that every person in your organization will at some point in the year come across a potential business lead that your sales team would be interested in. Yet I have worked with companies where they say they have 'no leads' yet have 100 people on clients' sites every day. All teams who interact with customers need to be educated on what a 'lead' is to the company and then inspire them to share those leads with the business development teams.

4: Pitch process

Sales professionals were once masters of their own destiny in a pitch process; in today's sales process they must rely on accountants, lawyers, operations, procurement, marketing and others to help convert opportunities into deals. The challenge is that sales professionals are often asking for help from individuals who have other responsibilities on top of helping with them with pitch processes. The challenge for organizations is that sales teams are used to demanding support and not having to sell internally to get the support they need.

5: Account expansion

It is accepted that it is easier to win more business from an existing client than to find and win a new client, yet many sales professionals are protective of their client relationships. This is often at the expense of the wider organization's sales growth and to the detriment of their clients. The challenge for companies is how to motivate and inspire greater levels of cross selling across different teams.

The self-interest and collaboration dilemma

Cross selling may make sense intellectually, but when self-interest, inter-departmental rivalry and a client's best interests come into play, things can get complicated.

Yet how managers address and tolerate uncollaborative behaviour can deeply affect motivation levels across a team and organization.

Self-interest and interdepartmental rivalry are a double-edged sword for sales teams. On the one hand, self-interest unlocks high levels of discretionary effort to go above and beyond the norm to achieve success, which of course we like. The downsides of self-interest come about, however, when it becomes a dominant sales culture trait. You can see the extreme examples in movies such as *The Wolf of Wall Street* and *Wall Street*. In these movies the whole organizational culture was focused towards self-interest.

Collaboration doesn't mean there can't be healthy levels of competition. Interdepartmental or inter-team rivalry generates a collective desire to beat other teams. When the competition is at healthy levels, it creates a sales culture where individuals work well together and support each other as they work towards their collective targets. However, just as the potential win is far greater, the consequences of poor collaboration can be significant.

Most sales leaders reading this book will have come across consultants who are driven by self-interest. Netflix calls this profile the 'brilliant jerks.'[1] In their book *The Challenger Sale*, Brent Adamson and Matthew Dixon[2] call them 'lone wolfs'. More often, they are described as the ones you cannot afford to lose and so organizations tolerate the negative behaviours. In many instances, those managers spend their days putting out fires created when self-interest overtakes the client or organizational benefit. It never ceases to amaze me the level of motivational damage that can be caused, both internally and externally, by an individual whose self-interest exceeds their interest in the company, peer or customer's needs. The challenge comes when this type of self-interested individual is a top performer, as the company's leadership is torn between values and financial gain.

James Kerr's book *Legacy* (2013)[3] makes some very interesting points about the principles of the All Blacks rugby team that makes its culture so effective. Notably, there is the 'No Dickhead' policy as part of the team's pursuit of the whanau (whanau is an extended family or community of related families who live together in the same area). But in the business world leaders are torn between two options. Do you take the money generated and accept a dilution of your values or do you stand by your values and demand a change in behaviour? And if it does not happen, go one step further and remove the person from your business? What choice would you make if you had a top biller with toxic behaviours? In theory the choice is an easy one to make, but faced with a large hole in your budget, the right thing is often the hardest thing to do.

What are the options to solve the sales collaboration puzzle?

Traditional approaches to encouraging sales collaboration tend to involve competitions, compensation and recognition. Once or twice a year, companies may have a big push on cross selling services between teams or lead generation for other parts of the organization with success being rewarded with a holiday, iPad, extra holiday days and so on. The challenge with this approach is that it infers collaboration is a temporary state of mind rather than an everyday state. Using compensation to motivate cross selling or collaboration works in many instances (after all, who would not want to earn a bonus for flipping a lead?), but there's a problem in that the extra compensation is usually marginal in comparison to individual commission payments. In addition, it reduces collaboration to a commercial transaction.

While incentivizing collaborative behaviour through competitions and compensation can work, it assumes that the primary motivators of sales professionals are money and physically orientated rewards, such as iPads, holidays etc. It also sends out a message that to be collaborative, individuals should be given something extra, on top of their standard compensation. Surely, the goal of a core value is that it is part of the everyday principles that all employees sign up to?

Some organizations try to improve collaboration by building in systems and processes to recognize those individuals that do collaborate well and are seen to be living the values of the organization. 'Employee Recognition; Low Cost, High Impact', a 2016 Gallup news story published on the back of Gallup research, talks about how important employee recognition is and how little of it goes on.[4] According to Gallup's findings, only one in three of the US workers polled strongly agreed that they had received recognition or praise for doing good work in the preceding seven days. There was good news from the research though: it found that the most memorable recognition usually comes from an employee's manager (28 per cent), followed by a high-level leader or CEO (24 per cent), the manager's manager (12 per cent), a customer (10 per cent) or peers (9 per cent).

This research indicates that employee recognition is an effective and inexpensive way of rewarding people and reinforcing behaviour that reflects an organization's core values. When the survey respondents were asked what forms of recognition were most memorable, the answers showed that money isn't everything.

The six most common responses were:

- public recognition or acknowledgement via an award, certificate or commendation;
- private recognition from a boss, customer or peer;

- high level of achievement in reviews or evaluations;
- promotion or increase in work responsibilities;
- monetary award such as a bonus, prize or base salary increase;
- personal satisfaction or pride in work.

Concept applied

The technology solutions company, Brother UK, has a brilliant way of incentivizing collaborative behaviour. They have created a peer-to-peer recognition system, that allows employees of all levels to recommend a colleague for further recognition when they have gone the extra mile. While the awards are not significant from a financial perspective, they have a significant impact on the individuals who receive them. Who would not like a colleague sharing with the company that you had gone 'above and beyond'? The key to the success of this programme is that the time between recommendation and awarding of the award is no more than 24 hours so that the moment doesn't fade and excellence gets locked in.

While a pat on the back from the CEO can be effective, my belief is that even the most individually centric sales professionals do share and collaborate, although that collaboration is often conditional. They want to know that the teams and individuals they are working with, or introducing their clients to, are professional, credible and likely to deliver a service equal to or better than the one they would deliver.

If you ask one of your sales team 'Why do you not collaborate more?' you are unlikely to receive an answer that directly states that the person or team dislikes working with other people or teams. The most likely excuse given by the sales consultant is 'I do not think it is in the best interests of the client' or 'My client does not want to be called by other people.' It always makes me smile when I hear this excuse. The individual is likely good enough at relationship building to find prospective clients and nurture the relationship through to closing a sale, but unable to convince the client that their colleague may be worth talking to. A likely story...

Let's imagine a scenario: you are a stockbroker and you have a client who needs some advice to help manage income planning for retirement. You have a choice to recommend Steve – your colleague who works for your financial planning service; you have heard he is a good guy but have not met him yourself – or to recommend Sian – who works for a local financial planning consultancy, whom you have met and whose work you know is highly regarded. Or you could just leave the client to find someone on their own. While you know the stockbroker's sales manager will have a preference on which choice should be made, the reality is that the decision is the stockbroker's to make. This is because it is unlikely the manager will speak to the client personally and discuss what options were presented to them. The choice is made at the discretion of the sales consultant.

The subtext to this scenario is that the sales professional does not feel comfortable in the capabilities of the colleague they will be introducing. The best way to improve collaboration between teams and individuals is to focus on building confidence, credibility and trust between all parts of the business development and delivery process. When teams and individuals know each other better, they are more likely to share knowledge and work collaboratively.

Below are some examples of conversations that managers can facilitate between the different teams that contribute to the business development function.

How do you encourage your sales, marketing and operations teams to become more collaborative?

The first step for any attempt to improve collaboration is an open and honest discussion around what is and is not collaborative behaviour. Then conversations and discussions can progress to increasing understanding between teams and building stronger relationships. Here are some exercises and discussions that will help facilitate discussions between individuals and teams to improve familiarity and confidence in each other's capability.

Collaboration within the leadership team

Sales leaders are the individuals that deal with the day-to-day challenges that come with managing a group of people who are largely motivated by self-interest, interpersonal and inter-departmental rivalry. When there are differences between leaders on what is and is not collaborative behaviour, it has the potential to create long-lasting personal and team grudges. Left to fester, these grudges create inefficiencies and open opportunities for competitors to steal clients and market share. What is required is a consistent approach to collaboration from sales leaders and a consistent approach to dealing with disputes around collaborative behaviour.

Below are discussion topics that senior leaders can engage their leadership team in.

a) Quit trash talking colleagues and teams

One way that sales leaders build individual confidence and team spirit is by trash talking other individuals or teams within the organization. It could be anything from 'credit control are useless' to 'no one in that office knows what they are talking about'. Irrespective of whether these statements are true or not, they set the tone for the whole team's interaction with those departments or individuals. They also reduce a team's desire or willingness to collaborate. Managers should temper the criticism of other individuals or functions, rather than fuel it.

Discussion question

How can reducing the trash talking of other teams or individuals improve confidence and trust in other parts of the organization?

---

b) Manage conflict proactively

The nature of sales teams and how they work invariably means that there is conflict between individuals and teams. However, it is how managers manage this conflict that determines whether a situation is a blip in a relationship or a lifelong grudge. While some managers are great at dealing with conflict within their own teams, conflict with outside teams can stretch their capability. The goal of this discussion question is to encourage managers to agree a way of dealing with inter-team conflict in a more positive way.

Discussion question

How can we change how we deal with inter-team conflict to maintain confidence and trust between teams?

---

c) Recognize success

Sales professionals are typically very motivated by public recognition. However, the challenge with collaboration is that most collaborative activity cannot be directly linked to sales success. Most collaboration will involve sharing nuggets of market knowledge, giving advice on the fly or connecting people together. So how does an organization recognize these little contributions? The purpose of this discussion is to get your leadership team to think about how they can recognize collaboration more frequently.

Discussion question

How can we better recognize the many little acts of collaboration we witness day in, day out?

What stops us collaborating?

The challenge leaders face when addressing a lack of collaboration is that they are often hard pushed to find anyone in their team who would say 'I am not collaborative.' More often their team grudgingly commits to being more collaborative. However, what these discussions often lack is an open and frank discussion on what is and is not collaborative behaviour. This is because in these discussions they quickly descend into finger pointing and individuals justifying their behaviour based on what someone else had done in the past or to them directly. The aim of these discussion questions is to actively engage in discussion of situations that are often the catalyst for uncollaborative behaviour.

Discussion 1: What happens when we...?

The key to promoting collaboration is for everyone to understand what collaborative behaviour should take place in any situation. Any lack of clarity or broad-brush understanding will leave room for a sales consultant to say 'I did not know that was required.' That's why you and your team need clarity on how to behave in different situations so that they can make the right decisions. For example, if I pick up a lead for another team, what should I be expected to do when passing it over? Email over the name of the company and contact? How quickly? If I have insight on the organization concerned, should I share what I know? The purpose of this discussion exercise is to clarify what should happen in any given situation.

Discussion exercise

Preparation: Prepare a list of situations when you expect your team to be collaborative.

Discussion: Follow this three-step process as many times as you wish. After each step stop and facilitate answers (remember if there are issues not being brought up, bring them up yourself).

Step 1: Ask: What happens when we <insert situation>? How can we be collaborative to help <insert team or person>?

Step 2: Ask: What stops us doing this?

Step 3: What can we do to resolve these problems / issues that stop us collaborating?

Discussion 2: What happens when they...?

While most salespeople understand how they need to collaborate with other people and teams, sometimes it is the behaviour of individuals or teams that leads to uncollaborative behaviour. This discussion is an opportunity to clarify what your team should do when other teams are not as collaborative as they should be.

The challenge for a sales leader is knowing how to engage their sales teams in resolving the issue with another individual or team rather than perpetuating it. This exercise is designed to help managers engage their teams in positive discussion to resolve an uncollaborative relationship.

Discussion exercise

Preparation: Prepare a couple of examples of where teams or individuals have been uncollaborative with you and your team.

Discussion: Follow this three-step process as many times as you wish. After each step stop and facilitate answers (remember if there are issues not being brought up, bring them up yourself).

Step 1: Ask: When <insert name or individual or team> did this <insert situation> how did it make us feel? What would we like to do in return?

Step 2: Say and ask: Now with our collaborative heads on, how should we respond?

Step 3: Ask: What can we do to stop this happening in the future?

Discussion 3: Expand your client base

The skill of the professional is being able to put to one side what they feel to build a constructive two-way relationship with their client. Frustratingly for leaders who want to build collaborative environments, they may have many individuals in their teams who struggle to do this with internal relationships.

A parallel I often use with sales teams is the similarity between a sales consultant and a Formula One driver. In Formula One motor racing, all the kudos goes to the driver. However, it takes over 300 people behind the scenes to get two competitive cars on the track. During the race, you have a 13-person pit crew just to change the wheels. There are engineers managing the performance of the engine and individuals back at base reviewing the competing teams' activities, looking for rule infringements.

It's a similar scenario in a sales team. The kudos goes to the sales consultant, but more and more, there's a team of people behind them, helping convert leads into tenders and tenders into deals won. The purpose of the following exercises is to help sales teams have a greater awareness of how many people support them in winning a deal.

Discussion exercise

Being aware of your support team

Step 1: Map your sales process

On a whiteboard or using sticky notes, ask your team to map out your sales process from beginning to end. As you map the process, ensure you cover every stage of the process, from research and branding through to service delivery and account management. This is important because sales professionals often see the sales process as being just the parts they are involved in, rather than a longer, broader process.

Step 2: Identify the support network

Using sticky notes, ask individuals to add how different functions support at different stages of the process (tip: have a list of different functions for reference). Ask the group to explain in more detail what role a particular function plays in supporting the process and how it contributes to success as a whole.

Step 3: Supporting your supporters

Picking a stage and function at random, ask two questions:

- What are the things that this team could do to make the sales team's life harder if they chose to?

- If they wanted to go the extra mile, how could this person or team help you hit your target?

NOTE The point of this stage is that the sales team begins to discuss how support functions have a choice about how hard they want to work to support sales and help them to succeed.

Step 4: Building a new client base

Now is the time to get your team to think about building a list of individuals internally that they need support from to succeed. Ask them to write a list of the top three or five people that they need to build better relationships with then add two or three things they can do on the next 30 days to help build or strengthen their relationships.

Who needs what?

You could assume that sales teams and those supporting the sales teams are fully aware of each other's needs and this assumption may well hold at the top level. However, when it comes to the little details of knowledge or activity that teams need from each other every day, it may well prove otherwise. How many sales are booked with incorrect company billing details, target customers tagged with incorrect data or potential leads for other teams overlooked because someone, somewhere, did not fully understand what constitutes a lead for a different team in the organization? I had a research meeting with a CEO recently when he explained that they had issues with the sales team promising clients things during the sales process that were possible but created significantly more work for the implementation team. Importantly, this was not deliberate anti-collaborative behaviour, but more a case of the sales professional offering sweeteners to a client to secure the deal, without realizing the impact on the teams following behind.

The following exercises are all designed to help managers increase understanding between peers, sales, marketing and other support teams. There are subtle differences between them, in that they focus on different ways to share understanding of what individuals need to do to succeed and to increase the awareness of the challenges they face in doing their jobs.

What do my leads look like?

Great sales consultants typically focus on having a pre-existing relationship with a client before they have a need to buy. While a lead to someone who is looking to buy a product or service right now is always gratefully received, it is information indicating a change in a client's circumstances that may lead to a need in the next 60/90/180 days that is often of the greatest value. There may be a fairly consistent understanding of what an immediate lead looks like across the organization, but the understanding of future need leads is often less clear and differs from team to team. This means teams often dismiss information as irrelevant but which is, in fact, valuable to another team.

Discussion exercise

What is a lead to me?

Note: This meeting can be conducted as a group discussion or as an individual presenting to another team or support function.

Preparation: Sales professional to prepare three lists of different types of leads. On these lists they could write the change, issues and challenges they may see in a company that could indicate a future opportunity.

List 1: Hot leads that need chasing urgently (ie currently or imminently in pitch process with competitors).

List 2: Warm leads indicate there could be an opportunity to pitch in the next 90 days (ie covering an issue internally, project running over schedule).

List 3: Cool leads indicate there could be an opportunity to pitch in the next 180 days (ie new CEO, CMO or merger).

Step 1: Present

Sales professional presents their lists to either another sales team or support function taking time to explain how they may either gain the relevant knowledge or situations where they may encounter clients with challenges that may result in future needs.

Step 2: Engage

Ask those listening two questions:

- What extra support could I give you to help you understand what a lead could be?
- What can I do for you in return for your help?

This last question is key for the sales consultant to showing they see their relationship as a two-way process.

A day in their shoes

If you ever get the chance to work at Honda you will be lucky enough to experience a week on the car production line. Or if you work at OVO Energy, once a year you will need to spend a day on the phones as a customer service agent, experiencing the situations and conversations that customer service agents handle every day. Why? The goal is that by doing the job of someone you depend on, you will better understand the challenges they face and appreciate the role you play in helping them do it. If you cannot spare individuals being taken away from their day job, then a halfway house is having individuals sit together while they do their day job.

I once had issues between a sales team and a credit control team. At the heart of the problem was a lack of understanding of each other's role. I arranged for credit control to work on the same bank of desks as the sales consultants. They spent their day collecting money specifically related to that team. During the day there was a continual flow of questions from the credit controller to the sales team. The questions were about payment terms agreed, company addresses, invoice dates and more. By the end of the day the sales consultants were much more aware of the issues the lack of data on the CRM caused and, more importantly, they had got to know the credit controller as a person rather than an anonymous person sitting in a shared service centre. The result: collaboration was improved and both teams became more effective.

Exercise

A day in their shoes

This not so much an exercise for you to run with others but one to run with yourself. All you need to do is to answer the following question, list the names and think about how you could make it happen:

Question: Which sales consultant / support function would benefit from following <insert person/team> for a day?

Summary

Collaboration is one of the most important values for companies wanting to create an organization-wide approach to business development. As with many chapters it deserves a book of its own. However, the focus for this chapter has been on helping the sales team wanting to collaborate with each other and the wider organization. There is no doubt in my mind that, in a fast-changing world where the traditional sales process is changing dramatically, the 'lone wolf' will find it harder and harder to succeed.

References

1 Schleckser, J (2016) *Why Netflix doesn't tolerate brilliant jerks* https://www.inc.com/jim-schleckser/why-netflix-doesn-t-tolerate-brilliant-jerks.html [last accessed 14/4/18]

2 Dixon, M and Anderson, B (2012) *The Challenger Sale: How to take control of the customer conversation*, Portfolio Penguin

3 Kerr, J (2013) *Legacy*, Constable

4 Mann, Annamarie and Dvorak, N (2016) *Employee Recognition: Low cost, high impact* http://news.gallup.com/businessjournal/193238/employee-recognition-low-cost-high-impact.aspx [last accessed 14/4/18]

How to build confidence and capability   11

KEY CHAPTER TAKEAWAYS

- Aligning customer, company and individual purpose.
- How to sync the sales process with learning and development strategy.
- By having confident, capable individuals and teams, companies can achieve successful business development and lasting cultural change.
- Managers can become better at-desk coaches to increase confidence and capability.

This whole book is about inspiring confidence in your teams to really engage in performing their jobs to the very best of their abilities. Much of what we have focused on so far has aimed at building an environment where everyone believes in the wider goals of the organization and the benefits that a product or service delivers to the customer. We have discussed what might make people feel better about what they do, but it does not guarantee that they will be doing everything required of them to hit their targets. The key challenge for organizations is how they sustain high levels of motivation in their sales team when what has always been a challenging job is getting even more challenging.

I regularly hear sales directors talk about the difficulty of finding people with the right capabilities. I normally respond by asking

'What about developing your own talent?' The response varies but, commonly, directors say it is increasingly difficult to find raw talent and develop those people to a level of productivity as quickly as is needed. How long it takes to develop a new person who has no experience will vary business by business, but let's take the recruitment sector as an example. In recruitment, it takes 18 to 24 months to develop someone to the point where they can perform consistently at a self-sufficient level. This is a long time to wait for self-sustaining performance and it means that from the outset both the company and the new sales professional are pushing hard for success. Both parties will be stretching for results and pushing for high levels of capability growth. The challenge is that when companies and individuals push for quick results, it makes the fall even greater should those results not be achieved and individuals lose faith.

Let's think of it a different way. If you sign up for a half marathon or a triathlon, you will probably set yourself a target time. As you train you hope that your training times will begin to show that you will meet your target. The harder you train, the more expectation you have that you will hit your performance goal. What you are looking for is little milestones that indicate that you are going to hit your target, with each little success boosting your confidence and belief that you will hit your goal. When I was training for a half marathon, it was about being able to run longer every week before my knee started to hurt. But how do you feel if, after three months of giving it everything, you are still way off track? When chasing my half marathon, for example, three months into training I had yet to achieve a single seven-minute mile let alone run 13 miles back to back. Would you keep going at the same level of intensity or would you adjust your goal? How would you feel if after another three months you were still way off track? Would your belief start to waver? In our personal lives, if we are going to miss a goal we adjust our targets and focus on hitting the new goal. In the workplace, however, every time you feel you are not meeting your manager's expectations or your own expectations, you expend some of your belief in your capabilities. The harder you try, the greater the amount expended and if a person runs out of belief altogether, it is only a matter of time before you fire them or they fire themselves.

The greatest loss for businesses is not when new sales consultants leave after three months, but when consultants switch careers or take a career break after 12 to 15 months. Losing new sales consultants at this stage is tremendously disappointing for the business, the manager and the individual, not least because managers are often happy with the individual's level of performance and can see higher performance on the horizon. It's the individuals themselves who don't see this and once their belief that they will hit their targets has gone, they are on the road to resigning.

My experience of working with thousands of new sales professionals over many years tells me that it is this loss of belief that they will hit their goals that will cause them to leave. I see them in their first few weeks, eyes bright, full of passion and belief that they have made the right career choice and as the months progress you see those bright eyes fade away as the person agonizes over what they are doing with their career.

Managers need to focus on building up employee confidence levels and sustain a level of belief until their capability can support a consistent level of performance. One of my favourite images I show managers is the image in Figure 11.1 of a positive and negative cycle of motivation and demotivation. The purpose of showing it is to encourage managers to see the impact of developing both confidence and capability.

The modern manager has a lot on their plate though and there are some practical challenges that managers must deal with day to day

Figure 11.1 Positive and negative cycle of motivation

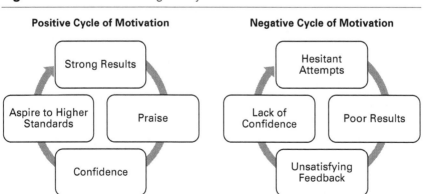

that impact their ability to develop individual and team confidence and capability. Examples of two challenges that managers have to overcome are discussed below.

1: *Phone reluctance*

Back when I started my first career job, my manager said to me on day one 'Alex, remember the phone is your friend. It is here to help you achieve your goals.' He said this because the phone was my primary tool when initiating and nurturing relationships. Yes, face-to-face meetings were important, but the phone was the key to securing those meetings. In today's world there are many more tools available. We now have email, Skype and Slack, for example, and an ever-expanding range of social networks that enable client identification and engagement and the ongoing nurturing of relationships. The challenge facing managers is that the phone is no longer perceived as a friend. In fact, the current zeitgeist is that cold calling people on the phone is a bad thing to do. This mentality can lead to sales professionals lacking confidence when making sales calls. The issue is that the younger cohort of sales professionals are digital natives and naturally turn to digital options before they turn to the phone.

This can cause tension between manager and sales consultant. On the one hand you have managers looking at their teams tapping away on email or cruising social media, thinking 'I want my teams on the phone more. If they don't speak to enough people, they will not get enough leads.' On the other hand, sales professionals may think their managers are dinosaurs that do not understand the digital world.

2: *Non-linear sales processes*

Ah… the simple days of sales scripts. Those days are long gone, or they should be. Often the modern sales process is not linear. Sales processes have become more complicated and they stretch over longer periods of time. The 'what should be done' and 'when' becomes a matter for the sales professional's judgement. The challenge for sales professionals is that when judgement is the determining success factor, confidence is slower to materialize as there is always something extra that could have been said or done. The impact of a non-linear process is that it is harder for trainers to teach decision making over process. The change that managers are having to make is to adapt their approach to training from being skills focused to the art of decision making with the goal of achieving self-sufficiency through the sales process. It can take longer to build confidence in a sales consultant's own decision making. This means managers need to provide ongoing training to support their teams making the right decision in the right situation.

Mapping competencies and capabilities is critical to success

The best way to lose the attention of a roomful of sales leaders (or anyone in fact!) is to stand up and say 'Let's talk about the competency framework.' You will have your own view of the word 'competencies'. I have always found it a word hard to connect with, probably because my early exposure to the term was associated with a list of broad behaviours such as communication, influence and team player. It all felt a little abstract. However, if when I was a sales manager, you had asked me to write down the things people needed to be able to do to succeed, you would have had 100 per cent of my attention. I would have been straight on the case!

Whether or not you call them competencies or capabilities, you can't knock the argument that having clarity on what individuals in your team need to do to succeed is key to having a successful sales team, whether you are executing or supporting the sales process. If you don't have a clear route map for success, it makes it harder for newbies to the team to understand the formula for success. It makes it much harder for the training team to support you and lastly, and most importantly, you lose access to one of the most useful tools for inspiring confidence and belief.

A capability framework allows both the individual and their manager to have an objective reference point to chart where and when capabilities are progressing. Seeing this progress in clear terms will also boost the self-belief of the sales consultant. The framework can also be used to assist performance management conversations and to highlight areas for improvement.

On my first day in sales I was presented with a list that the company called 'the recipe'. On this list were the skills and capabilities I needed to develop in order to stand a chance of succeeding. The question I always ask sales leaders is 'If I started today, how easy would it be for me to learn what I needed to do to succeed?'

How you make the idea of competencies work in your own head will be unique to you. However, here are some of the tactics I and other companies have used to increase buy-in to a competency/capability/skills framework.

1: Create a common language

You must create a language that works for you; who cares if you call it one thing but the rest of the world calls it another? The most important thing is that you and your managers buy in to the term and why it has been chosen. I have worked through several permutations over the years and have now settled on the term 'capability map'. Why? Firstly, it carries less baggage than the term 'competence', secondly, I think the term creates a positive intent in the mind of the manager or coach, ie 'are they capable of…?' 'how can I help them be more capable?', and thirdly and more importantly, I find that capabilities are likely to be statements defining a person's ability to achieve a desired outcome from a situation or activity. This allows the organization to then define 'what good looks like' in each area of capability and to build a list of skills that need to be taught.

Quick tip

If you want your managers to be more engaged in the listing of skills or activities that their teams need to succeed, then give them responsibility for naming it. If they feel they have shaped what it is called and how it works, they are more likely to engage with the implementation. This may not please your L&D or HR team, who may already use the term 'competency framework' or 'success drivers', but it is so important that managers have ownership of the capability map, or whatever you call it.

2: Explain 'WHY'

Typically, competency frameworks are great at telling you what you need to do but they are not so great at explaining 'WHY' this capability is important to success. If you are expecting your sales consultants to exercise judgement on the fly, it is critical that you help them understand 'WHY' what they must do will help them succeed or how not doing something will help them fail. In this sense, it is very like being a parent. While I know why I want my child to act or behave in a certain way, I can be guilty of saying 'Do this or don't do that' and forgetting to explain why. A tip that I once read for managing your child's behaviour better (let's face it – some days you run out of ideas!) was to be more proactive in explaining 'why' after you ask them to do something or after something has happened. The idea is that it begins to change your child's thought process from 'feel then do' to a thought process of 'feel, think, do', in essence, inserting consequence into the decision-making process. Does it work? Not always, but at least you have a strategy for progress. If you apply the same approach to developing individuals in your team, focusing on the why, the greater the likelihood that the right decision will be made at the moment of need.

Self-assessment questions

- How well does our training help newer sales consultants understand 'WHY' they are asked to do things?
- How good are managers at explaining 'WHY' things are done when coaching sales consultants at desk?

3: Systems capabilities

One of the biggest changes for sales professionals in the last eight years has been the need to learn and master a far wider range of IT systems than in the past. Whereas 10 years ago, most sales professionals just had to learn how to use their CRM to log sales activity or update the sales pipeline, now CRMs have a far greater capacity to enable higher levels of sales performance. In addition, there is a need for sales professionals to find and use new sales tools all the time. The challenge is that IT training is seen as a separate entity from sales training. Yet, technology is a significant enabler of a more efficient process. Unfortunately, many firms are not integrating technology usage into their capability framework to guide best practice and sales performance. The pressure is increasingly on managers to understand the different tech tools available to their team and integrate them into the sales process and coach their team to maximize the benefit from each tool.

Self-assessment questions

- How well documented are the IT/system capabilities a sales consultant needs to master to succeed?
- How well integrated is IT/systems training within the sales training framework?

4: Map and match

In the previous section of the book, I suggested a couple of exercises to look at your customers' buying process and compare it to your sales process. The aim was that you would be better able to target your sales and marketing activities to your clients' situation. Similarly, if you are in the process of changing your sales process, you need to re-map the capabilities your sales teams need to have in order to execute the process. Often when I suggest a re-mapping exercise to a sales director or CEO, I get the response 'Surely everyone already knows what to do. It is pretty straightforward.' I respond with 'How good are they at doing what they need to do at the moment?' The responses vary, but normally involve a 'could be better' or 'average'. At this stage, I suggest that either a large section of their team comes in to work every day and deliberately aims not to do what needs to be done, or there are a number of people who are unsure of what they need to do or why they need to do it. Call me naive, but I believe that the majority of people turn up every day to do a good job for their own benefit and the benefit of the company.

So, what is it that causes the disconnect between desired action and actual action? As demonstrated earlier, one answer is that companies do not promote 'why' things are done enough. Another reason is that the link between the sales process and what sales consultants are asked to do every day is not explicit enough which could be creating inefficiencies.

Self-assessment questions

Preparation: Before conducting this self-assessment, print a copy of your sales process, sales consultant job specification and/or competency framework.

- Read the job specification of the sales consultant. How well does it reflect what needs to be done by a sales consultant?
- Read the competency framework. How well does it reflect what capabilities need to be performed to successfully execute the sales process?

Continually evolving not static

Probably the biggest change in how I approach the use of capability maps in the last few years is to see them as living entities rather than a reflection on the past. Too often when you ask sales directors or HRDs when the last time a capability map was updated you get blank looks. The key to engagement is for the whole sales team to see the capability map as a living reflection of what people need to do to succeed in today's marketplace. Just as the leadership team adjusts tactics and approaches to grow marketing share, there should be a regular review of how the capabilities being taught match the skills needed to execute in today's marketplace.

Self-assessment questions

- When was the last time the competencies/capability framework updated?
- How could the competency framework be updated more frequently and involve a wider range of stakeholders?

Why managers should coach and train more

As markets rapidly evolve and processes become more complex, companies are having to look at sales training as an ongoing activity that continually improves how a sales professional approaches their job and equips them to deal with a broad range of situations. In accepting that individuals cannot spend weeks and weeks in training rooms, the responsibility for the ongoing development of sales teams is being passed to the sales manager. That's why sales managers now have to be both performance coaches and performance managers.

Despite this, I regularly encounter leaders of sales teams and CEOs who say 'My team needs sales training', followed immediately by an explanation of exactly what their team needs to be doing. My response is often that their team does not need training from me, but to be 'coached how to do their job from you'. This might sound like splitting hairs, but I strongly believe that external trainers should be brought in to an organization when managers have done everything in their power to educate their own team themselves and they need an injection of new ideas. The reason for this is that while managers may not be as effective as trainers, they will normally be experts in the situations their teams need to overcome to succeed.

A company that lives this philosophy is Procter & Gamble. A few years ago, I learnt from a director at Procter & Gamble that their approach to learning was that every leader was allocated responsibility for developing and delivering one training programme. The idea was that a director might own a course and have five or six senior managers allocated to them as part of an internal delivery team. Depending on the course, the senior managers were then supported by junior managers in the organization in delivering the training programme. Their belief was that getting managers and directors who were actually doing the job they were training people on, would preserve the company culture and inspire behavioural change much more than using external training providers or a team of internal trainers. An additional benefit of involving managers more in the development of their own staff is that the bond between manager and employee becomes stronger when the manager has played a significant role in developing an individual's capability.

However, just as organizations have learnt that great salespeople do not always make great managers, so great sales managers do not always make great sales coaches. A sales management role typically requires a heavy focus on managing work in progress and hitting targets, rather than developing people. You might think that one leads to the other and you are right in theory; however, you are more likely to hear about managers being fired for missing targets than being fired for being poor at developing people. This means sales managers are more likely to focus on results than an individual's capability development.

Also, in any leadership team, there will be a range of styles. Some managers are naturally very directive, while others are laissez-faire and many more are in-between. The default style of highly directive managers is to direct activities and tell people what to do and how to do it when they meet difficult situations. While this works on one level, it also creates teams that are great at doing what they are told but are not necessarily good at making their own decisions. On the other hand, laissez-faire managers are likely to either rely on individuals coming to ask for help, or believe that because they have told sales consultants what to do they will immediately be able to translate that new knowledge into action.

So, when a CEO stands up and says 'Our managers need to be better coaches', the intent may be a good one; however, the scale of the mindset shift needed by managers is often underestimated.

Increasing managers' coaching confidence

If you were asked by someone in sales for your top tips for success, what would you say? The chances are that you would have a philosophical statement or two (such as 'seek to understand before you seek to be understood),[1] then a sales model or two (such as SPIN selling), and finally some of your own tips and tricks that you know work.

It is no different for me after 20 years as a coach, trainer and consultant. I regularly get asked 'How can I be better at developing my team?' or 'How can I be a better coach?' So below are my top strategies for improving a manager's coaching capabilities.

1: *Selling and coaching are the same thing*

As a sales trainer there is one question I am asked more than any other. It is 'Do you miss selling?' My response? 'I am still in sales. The difference is that where I used to sell X, Y and Z, I now sell you on doing things differently.' The background to this statement is that in a sales role, you are not usually in a position to mandate what your client should do and when. You have to influence a client's decision making by showing how your product or service will get them where they want to go. If they listen to you, you have moved the chance of sale forward; if they do not, then you need to go back and work out another way of promoting your product or service that is better than other options currently open to them. Yes, I am a manager, coach and trainer, but I have always seen my job as being in sales still. My primary role in any of my management or training jobs has been to sell people on doing their jobs differently to help them achieve their goals. If I have a conversation and behaviour does not change, then the person I was helping has not bought the solution I was offering. My responsibility then as a sales coach is to work out why they did not buy what I was selling and then resell my solution differently.

Another parallel is that in a sales process, sales professionals fully expect their potential client to challenge the validity of the claimed benefits of a product or service. In fact, a large part of most training programmes is teaching salespeople how to handle objections and to see objections as buying signals. Yet when managers are trying to influence behaviour, they often see challenges from their staff on whether what they are being asked to do will work or not as unco-operative behaviour. In a sales process, a good sales professional would deliberately ask for potential issues as part of the trial closing process.

A key way to demystify coaching and training in the mind of the sales manager is to get them to think of it as a 'sale' rather than a management activity. If you can make this shift of mindset, the challenge of influencing behaviours and attitudes of individuals in your team suddenly becomes more achievable.

Concept applied

One of the most popular coaching frameworks taught to managers is the GROW technique. The GROW technique was born out of sports coaching and developed by Graham Alexander, Alan Fine and Sir John Whitmore. It was popularized by Alan Fine's *You Already Know How to Be Great*,[2] Sir John Whitmore's *Coaching for Performance*[3] and Max Landsberg's *The Tao of Coaching*[4]. The GROW Model[5] suggests that there are four stages in any coaching conversation. Firstly, there's establishing the Goal to provide focus, then discussing the Reality to define current reality and highlight the obstacles that need to be overcome. Thirdly, the Options stage asks the coach to discuss the various different ways that the gap between the Goal and Reality can be bridged and finally, the Way forward is agreed. The idea is that this approach to changing behaviour makes the process a two-way discussion, focused on achieving a desired outcome.

Figure 11.2   The GROW Model

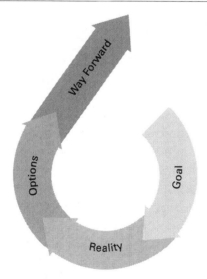

SOURCE The GROW Model graphic is © 2018 InsideOut LLC. Used with kind permission. For more information about the GROW Model and InsideOut GROW Coaching®, see insideoutdev.com

Sounding familiar? Is there a chance that it almost exactly mirrors the sales process?

Table 11.1   Similarities between sales conversation and GROW coaching conversation

	Sales conversation structure	GROW coaching conversation structure
Step 1	Build rapport – Get to know the person and what they want	Goal – Establish what the individual wants to achieve
Step 2	Find need/challenges – Learn what is stopping the customer getting what they want	Reality – What is stopping them achieving what they want to achieve?
Step 3	Present solution – Propose a solution matched against the highlighted needs	Options – Discuss the potential solutions available to solving the problems
Step 4	Close – Gain commitment to buy or move to the next stage of the sales process	Way forward – Agree an action plan to address and overcome challenges

The main difference between a sales conversation and a GROW coaching conversation is who drives the conversation. In a sales conversation with a client, it is the sales professional that is guiding the conversation towards their desired outcome. In my experience, great salespeople also play the role of a guide, helping the coachee 'discover' how the solution being presented is the best one for them. They are also willing to help the coachee choose someone else's solution if that's the best solution, ie invest in the long-term relationship. In a coaching conversation the 'coach' plays the role of a guide, helping the coachee find their own resolutions to their problems, and there you have it: you now have a team of managers who already understand 90 per cent of what a coaching conversation should be. The only challenge managers need to overcome is keeping their mouths shut and focus on getting the coachee to provide their own solutions.

Sales managers actually have an advantage over non-sales managers in the coaching process. Where non-sales managers can see the GROW process as a linear process that is followed from start to finish, sales managers know that a sales conversation is rarely linear. I would say the best managers display the same flexibility. They know that a question or objection may be raised at any point in the process, even during the closing phase and that query or objection may require them to go back to the finding the need stage in order to reclarify the client need, before progressing along the process once more.

2: Don't forget the little things that make up the big things

If I had a penny for every time I have heard a manager say 'I have told them what to do, but they are not doing it', I would be a wealthy man. Managers often explain tasks or actions that from their perspective require someone to go from A to get to B; however, when you think about the things that have to be considered when getting from A to B, from the perspective of the sales consultant it feels like they need to go from A to Z. When the sales consultant does not get the desired result, the manager will be frustrated; however, the manager is likely to have forgotten all the little lessons they had to master until life became as simple as A to B.

As a father I am continually reminded of this as I bring up my sons. Who would have thought that it would be so difficult to learn to eat properly at a table! But it is easy to forget all the little things I had to master to be considered someone that 'eats properly at a table', eg stay seated, do not shout, use cutlery, eat with your mouth closed… the list goes on. The key for me as a parent, or you as a coach, is to remember that once upon a time you needed to learn all the little things that enable you to make going from A to B or Z look easy.

The Conscious Competence Learning Model

This model was developed in the 1970s at Gordon Training International by one of its employees, Noel Burch.[6] The central premise behind the model is that we go through four stages as we learn:

- Unconscious incompetence: we do not know why we are bad at something.
- Conscious incompetence: I now know why I am bad at this thing.
- Conscious competence: I know that if I do this then this happens and I get the outcome I want.
- Unconscious competence: I do what works without thinking.

Figure 11.3   Conscious Competence Learning Model

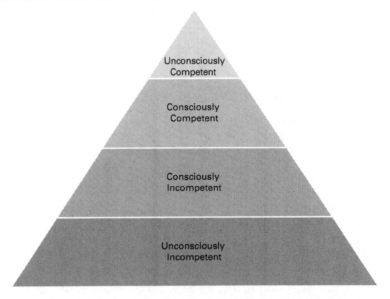

SOURCE Four Stages of Competence, Noel Burch (1977) Teacher Effectiveness Training (TET) Instructor Guide. Used with kind permission of Gordon Training International www.gordontraining.com

Let's apply this to the process of learning to drive:

Stage 1: We get in the car for the first time. We are excited, and we think we are going to be great. We are unconsciously incompetent.

Stage 2: We drive the car and realize that parking is not as easy as your parents made it look. You are consciously incompetent.

Stage 3: We learn tactics such as looking for reference points when reversing, and hey presto, we can park. We are consciously competent.

Stage 4: We have learnt what we need to do without thinking. We are unconsciously competent.

In the original 1970s version of this model it was a linear model, where you worked towards conscious competence as a pinnacle of learning (see Figure 11.3 above). However, in my own experience this process operates as a cycle (Figure 11.4) as the longer we are subconsciously competent, the more we work out that we can be

Figure 11.4   Conscious Competence Learning Cycle

SOURCE Four Stages of Competence, Noel Burch (1977) Teacher Effectiveness Training (TET) Instructor Guide (pages 4–14 and 4–15). Used with kind permission of Gordon Training International, www.gordontraining.com

more efficient and achieve the desired results by using shortcuts. In our minds we are still competent at what we do, until an event occurs that gets us to reflect on our state of competence.

Let's extend the driving analogy. You think you are in Stage 4. However, you know you are now taking short cuts on the best practice you learnt when you passed your test. After a few years, you start joking with your friends that 'I would not pass my test if I had to take it again today', yet you still think you are competent. You then get a speeding ticket and opt for the speed awareness course. You attend the course and suddenly, where you thought you were competent, you were actually unconsciously incompetent. The course must take you back to conscious competence.

It's the same in the work environment. You spend the first 12–18 months developing the skills you need to achieve your targets month in month out. In the following 12 months you still hit targets, but deep down you know you are taking short cuts. Suddenly an event happens, such as losing a big client or having a deal fall through or missing your targets two months in a row. You then sit down with your manager and talk through where things are going wrong. Kaboom, where you thought you were unconsciously competent you were in fact unconsciously incompetent. You then discuss with your manager all the things you used to do when you started being successful. You are now back in the zone of conscious competence and you are back on track. You leave the room motivated, with a plan to do the things you already knew how to do.

Managers often get frustrated when they have to teach the same things time and again to people in their teams. Understanding this approach to learning makes them less likely to become frustrated and helps them to focus on bringing their team member back to conscious competence.

3: Have an adaptable approach as one size does not fit all

Coaching and training does not suit a one-size-fits-all approach. Just as many managers go through the process of learning that you cannot manage everyone in your team the same way, the same goes for coaching and training. The content and tone of a coaching discussion will depend on a number of factors, with performance, experience and work ethic being a few of the determining ones. Sometimes you may be working with underperforming sales consultants where you may want to be direct in your approach; however, would this work on an experienced consultant whom you know can do the job well but is lacking motivation? In all likelihood you would adapt your approach. But how?

For a guide of what to do and when I always turn to the Skill/Will matrix (see Figure 11.5) introduced by Max Landsberg (2003).[7] The premise of the coaching model is that you should approach a coaching conversation according to both the skill level and the motivation level of the individual. In this model you have four categories of people:

High will and high skill: These individuals are called stars. In many instances, the manager's approach to coaching 'high will/high skill' individuals will be to delegate responsibilities and additional responsibilities (management or autonomy).

High skill and low will: These are often the stars of the past or ex-top performers who the manager knows can do better. The coaching approach for 'high skill/low will' individuals needs to focus on motivating the individual to re-engage with their own purpose of being at work. Hitting this individual with a KPI stick or sending them on 'back to basics training' is unlikely to increase motivation levels.

High will and low skill: This is often the sales rookie who is looking to make their mark. They may be low skill but their desire to learn makes them great to work with. The coaching approach focuses on increasing knowledge and recognizing the incremental steps of improvement they make week to week, month to month.

Low skill and low will: This is the individual who is not very capable and, more frustratingly, not working hard enough to improve their chances of success. In many sales teams you hear managers talking about the 'up or out' conversation. The coaching approach for this type of individual is to be direct with desired behaviours and outcomes.

This matrix is super easy to understand and managers can immediately begin to apply it to their teams. You can also assess a person as a whole or individual parts of their role. For instance, a person could be high will and high skill at account management but low skill and

Figure 11.5 The Skill/Will matrix

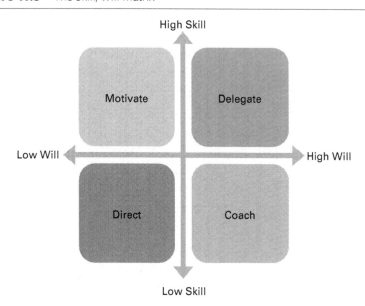

low will at new business development. Something to be mindful of is that the assessments are pretty subjective, so can be influenced by a manager's personal biases. Tread very carefully here to make sure this doesn't happen. However, for the purposes of a manager assessing how they should approach a coaching conversation, this model serves its purpose well.

4: Praise creates lasting behavioural change

Most work environments can be pretty unrelenting and praise can be in short supply. Research conducted by Gallup[8] found that less than one in three US workers received any praise from any supervisor or manager in the last seven years. However, when someone receives praise or recognition from a manager, supervisor or peer they start to feel good about what they are doing, which in turn makes them want to replicate the behaviours or actions where they received praise.

From a scientific perspective, when someone gets praise they receive a hit of dopamine in the brain. Dopamine is a highly addictive chemical that is produced by the part of the brain that processes reward and positive emotions. So, when your manager says 'Well done for closing that deal', the recipient is likely to get a hit of dopamine and, as dopamine is addictive, it is likely to lead to a desire to repeat the activity. The challenge is that in sales environments, praise is likely to be linked to closing a sale or hitting a target. This means that individuals can often go a while without any specific praise or recognition. Managers need to be more proactive in praising more of the little things that a sales consultant does that you know will contribute to their success. This may be something as mundane as having a detailed daily plan, or using a question you told them to ask or handling a difficult situation well. Doing this constructively is where the SBI approach to giving and receiving feedback comes in.

The Situation Behaviour Impact Model – Center for Creative Leadership[9]

Sometimes individuals in your team do things that just make you want to scream but you know that screaming will do little to change the situation or reduce the likelihood of the situation occurring again. Equally, when someone in your team does something good, just saying 'Well done, that was great' may well give the little boost you want them to feel, but if it is not connected to a specific action or behaviour, then the individual is unlikely to replicate their behaviour again. Whether you are looking to share positive or negative feedback with an individual or team, the more objective and specific the feedback, the more likely you are to influence a change in behaviour in the future. As with the best techniques or models, they do not need much explaining. The SBI feedback model (Situation-Behaviour-Impact), developed by the Center for Creative Leadership, is a simple and easy to apply approach to giving and receiving feedback.

Situation: Do you remember earlier today when you came back from the meeting?

Behaviour: You walked around the office talking to everyone to tell them how much you got from the meeting.

Impact: While your success was a positive thing to share, you distracted the team for 40 minutes because you didn't wait until lunchtime to share it with them.

In practice the S is intended to focus the mind of the person to the specific point in time. The B focuses on highlighting the action or behaviour and the 'I' provides the feedback (whether positive or negative). At this point, both the person giving and receiving feedback are focused on the same point in time and are thinking about the same action or behaviour. This opens up the possibility of feeding back the 'I' of that behaviour. Once delivered, it may open a larger conversation on how this behaviour can be replicated or avoided in the future. The key to this model is that both sides focus on the same thing at the same time.

One of the best things about this approach is that it also helps managers to plan conversations in advance, which can reduce the tension a manager feels when facing a tricky conversation.

5: Seek explanation not confirmation

As a manager I hated checking up on my team's activity and whether they had done what needed to be done. I do not like to be nagged or be the one nagging but that is what management represented to me after six months in the job. Then rather than asking my team confirmation questions all day like 'Have you chased that lead?' and 'Have you arranged those interviews?', I took a different approach.

I asked them explanation questions. I learnt what was gained from activities, rather than just checking whether they had been done. So rather than saying 'Have you chased that lead?' I was able to say 'What happened when you chased that lead?' I was still checking that a task had been done, but at the same time, I was finding out about that person's capability and I was also helping progress a lead to be an opportunity to pitch. This approach allows you to understand more about the situation the sales consultant encountered and assess how they dealt with it.

While the 'explanation not confirmation' approach has been effective over the years it has been hard to teach to other managers. However, a senior police officer on a train once told me about the Little TED questioning that is used for investigative questioning.

Little TED questioning

'Little TED' questioning involves three simple openings to knowledge-seeking questions:

T: Tell me.

E: Explain to me.

D: Describe to me.

To be a great performance coach you need to understand the why and the how, not just the what. The more you know the why and the how, the greater your understanding of an individual's capability to handle different situations. It helps you, as a manager, to be more targeted in your coaching advice. This approach also aligns with the principle that coaching is very similar to selling. A consultative approach to selling is generally more interested in how a client is feeling or why they made a decision, rather than just that the decision has been made. By understanding the why, the sales professional can work to influence future decision making. Coaching your team is no different, so try looking for explanations rather than confirmations.

6: Coaching at desk is better than in a meeting room

One of the largest drains on a billing manager's time is the ongoing questions they must answer from their team. All through the day your team asks questions and wants answers. One of the main reasons they do this is that they want your confirmation that they are doing the right thing. The challenge is that if you always give them the answer, they will take longer to build the confidence to make decisions for themselves. In many instances you know the person asking the questions knows the answer to the question they are asking, but just wants confirmation. This might be good for them but will impact the manager's ability to get their own job done.

In the moment training

This is a quick approach that I was taught while in my first job as a manager and still works well for me today. It goes like this: someone in your team asks you a question that you know they should be able to answer themselves. Your response goes like this:

Step 1: 'What are your options?' *Wait for options to be listed.*

Step 2: 'Which is the best one?' *Wait for answer.*

Step 3: Assuming the answer is a good one, you say 'Go for it!'

And that's it. What you are trying to achieve is breaking the habit of your team thinking you are the fountain of knowledge. You need to get them to start thinking for themselves. It may seem weird the first few times, but you will be amazed at how quickly your team either start making decisions for themselves or coming to you with a problem, the options and best option. And when that happens? You can just say 'Well done and go for it!'

Now there are two caveats to this approach. Firstly, there will be times when a deal is at risk and there is no time for a coaching conversation: you just need to be direct with your guidance. Over time these situations should lessen in frequency. Secondly, this approach focuses on getting your team to make decisions for themselves and sometimes they will make a decision and it will be the wrong one. While you may be frustrated that they have made the wrong call, focus on what they would do differently next time rather than criticizing them for doing the wrong thing. That is all there is to it. Enjoy the extra free time you are about to get!

7: Everyone can learn from everyone else

There are limits to the amount of coaching and training managers can do, that's why companies are increasingly taking a broader approach to capability development. Rather than focusing on building a training strategy, they are looking at developing the habit of learning within their organization. What I like about the term 'habit of learning' is that it implies learning is a continuous process. One of my favourite quotes is from Albert Gray, who wrote 'If you do not deliberately form good habits, then unconsciously you will form bad ones.'[10] It is all too easy for teams and individuals to fall into poor learning habits, particularly in a world where customers' needs change very quickly and your competition is adapting and changing every day. The need to continuously work to be better today than you were yesterday has rarely been greater. The phrase also implies that the habit of learning spreads the responsibility across the company, the organization's managers and the individuals themselves.

Companies with a strong learning culture are very effective at harnessing the wider knowledge held by employees by encouraging peer-to-peer sharing and learning. Many companies have created both formal and informal mentoring programmes, but others are going further. Companies are creating internal social networks where employees can go to solve challenges with their peers and while internal social networks might seem a strange concept, all it is really doing is mirroring how many of us approach our own personal learning

There are three approaches I see being used by companies looking to develop a learning culture:

1: Internal social networks

Tools like Slack, Chatter, Facebook Workplace or other social intranet tools make it much easier for peer to peer learning. These tools allow individuals to seek answers to problems and learn from the suggestions others make to solve problems they may also be experiencing. Importantly it enables ever more disparate workforces to learn without being in the classroom.

2: Leverage subject matter experts

Within small teams everyone normally knows who is the Excel expert, the CRM guru, or the person who is great at negotiations. However, as teams get larger and sometimes fragment into lots of smaller teams, awareness of who is good at what gets lost. A more organized approach to leveraging the capabilities of internal subject matter experts (SMEs) not only benefits the learner, but also provides a learning opportunity for the SME (such as future leaders or top billers). These individuals may grumble about not having the time to be involved in SME learning interventions, but the reality is that they love the recognition associated with being the expert of that topic. Future leaders benefit from an SME approach to learning; you may have individuals that are very keen to be managers but you feel they are not ready yet. Using these individuals as internal SMEs for training or coaching will develop those skills that are so critical to being a manager. It will also give you the opportunity to observe them and determine whether or not they are management material.

Collaborative team learning

We have already talked about collaboration in the previous chapter. However, I cannot exclude collaboration when writing about an organization's approach to learning.

What I mean by collaborative learning is that everyone in the team takes ownership for sharing ideas or strategies to help individuals improve performance. This could just be everyone being open to answering questions from newer sales consultants, or could be everyone finding and sharing content online that helps everyone stay current on trends in their industry. The key is that learning is more than sitting in a training room. It is about continually seeking ideas that help keep you and your team on top of your game.

Concept applied

For an example of social and collaborative learning, I know of a FTSE 50 company that has implemented a social learning platform where relevant industry articles are shared and discussed regularly. All sales professionals are encouraged to upload short videos of themselves overcoming objections or video snippets from client meetings (with client permission). The outcome is that, aside from the shared learning benefits, there has been more collaboration between sales consultants across sales regions and more active support of colleagues that are having challenges with clients or sales situations. A side outcome has been new sales consultants reach productivity quicker. The Head of Sales feels this is mainly due to training being delivered in smaller bite-sized chunks and the social platform enabling new individuals to learn from peers.

Summary

Overcoming employee reluctance to be involved in sales or marketing activity is a challenge all companies face. A key part of the solution is to increase the confidence and capability of those being expected to business develop and by applying the approaches in this chapter you will be able to increase both confidence and capability of your team.

References

1 Covey, S (2004) *7 Habits of Highly Effective People*, Simon and Schuster

2 Fine, A and Merrill, R (2010) *You Already Know How To Be Great*, Piatkus

3 Whitmore, J (1992) *Coaching for Performance*, Nicholas Brealey Publishing

4 Landsberg, M (2003) *The Tao of Coaching: Boost your effectiveness at work by inspiring and developing those around you*, Profile Books, London

5 The GROW Model graphic, © 2018 InsideOutLLC. Used with permission. For more information about the GROW Model and InsideOut GROW Coaching see insideoutdev.com

6 Burch, N (1977) *Four Stages of Competence*, in Teacher Effectiveness Training (TET) Instructor Guide (pages 4–14 and 4–15)

7 Landsberg, M (2003) *The Tao of Coaching: Boost your effectiveness at work by inspiring and developing those around you*, Profile Books, London

8 http://news.gallup.com/businessjournal/25369/praise-praising-your-employees.aspx

9 Center for Creative Leadership, *Feedback That Works: How to build and deliver your message* (website https://www.ccl.org/)

10 Gray, A E N, *The Common Denominator of Success* http://www.amnesta.net/mba/thecommondenominatorofsuccess-albertengray.pdf

Successful performance management in a business development context

12

KEY CHAPTER TAKEAWAYS

- How the leadership team approaches performance management is key to building the right business development culture.
- The best approach to performance management is this: the more people achieve, the more independence you give them.
- How to use review meetings to boost motivation.

We've all heard the quote 'People leave managers not companies' and we probably all agree with it. Gallup research agrees. In its *State of the American Workplace* report (2017), Gallup interviewed 7,200 adults and found that 50 per cent of employees have left a job 'to get away from their manager to improve their overall life at some point in their career'.[1]

Gallup's CEO, Jim Clifton, summed up the situation when he said 'The single biggest decision you make in your job – bigger than all the rest – is who you name manager. When you name the wrong person manager, nothing fixes that bad decision. Not compensation, not benefits – nothing.'[2] Performance management touches every part of the day-to-day running of a business development team.

The challenge companies face is how to balance the need to hit revenue and profit targets with how they treat their employees and customers. If a leadership team pushes too hard on revenue numbers it can create negative behaviours. Those negative behaviours can adversely affect customers, who feel that the sales team is being too pushy. They can also reduce motivation levels of sales teams, who feel there is too much pressure on them to 'close sales'. However, if you remove all targets and KPIs, would the sales team put in enough quality activity to yield the right level of sales results? It's a perennial balancing act that creates a number of challenges.

When most people think of motivating salespeople they think of trips abroad, bonuses and evenings in the pub. These incentives form the carrot approach. The other approach is, of course, the stick: fear. In every business development-type role, there is an implicit consequence of what will happen if you fail to hit your target: you might lose your job. Even in consulting and law firms, where partners may not be full-time business developers, there is an accepted assumption that careers do not progress if you cannot bring in business and grow your practice. One of my favourite sayings is 'Fear is like fire: if you manage it right it will keep your house warm all winter; let it get out of control it will burn your house down.'[3] The challenge for companies is that individuals fear unemployment less than they did 20 or 30 years ago. People have much more confidence now that they will find a new job, should they lose their current one. And employers don't expect people to stay put in one company for years on end any more. I regularly hear of sales professionals resigning without having another job lined up or leaving a job to go travelling 18 months into their career.

Another challenge for companies is that the traditional performance levers do not work so well any more. Traditionally, sales cultures were defined by an organization identifying the operating model and then managing people in such a way that they knew exactly what they should do and how they should do it. This was typified by managers using the phrase 'My way or the highway'. This worked when individuals believed that this was the way to be successful and were primarily motivated by money.

This approach doesn't appear to work so well anymore. I am regularly confronted by clients who say 'I cannot get salespeople or consultants that want to work hard. In my day...' What these managers are saying is that they cannot find people who are willing to work their way. Why? Because, as we have discussed, people want to work differently in today's workplace. This change in mindset is particularly evident in a sales team dominated by individuals in their 20s. While it would be easy to point the finger at millennials, I believe that the change is greater than just this cohort. I believe it reflects how the workforce as a whole now wants to operate at work.

So what is the answer? Sadly, there is no simple answer to solving the performance management puzzle. Consulting firms such as Deloitte and tech companies such as SuccessFactors are launching tools and frameworks to improve performance management. However, I can find no evidence that these challenges have yet been solved.

However, a number of companies are applying a series of principles to improve their approach to performance management. The goals of these principles are to:

- align company, employee and client interests;
- build an ability to flex the performance management approach based on individual performance;
- make one-to-one review meetings motivational;
- establish a broader approach to recognition;
- develop a proactive approach to underperformance.

Defining what you care about when managing performance

At the heart of motivational performance management is individuals believing your intent is true. What I mean by 'true' is that they believe that you are genuinely interested in helping them get what they want from being at work while you get what you and the company wants.

Probably the best example of this in practice is in the British military. At the Royal Military Academy, Sandhurst their motto is 'serve to lead'. It sounds like a paradox, but the two seemingly distinct qualities are interdependent. This motto focuses on an officer's ability to lead in an unselfish way. I learnt about it through my father, who spent over 15 years as an officer in the British Army. He described it to me as 'Your soldiers know that the objective of taking the hill is not negotiable. However, if they think your plan does not explicitly aim to bring as many as possible back home again, you may find yourself standing alone when it matters.'

So how does this apply to everyday life for those of us not in the army? Well, part of the emotional contract of employment is that we trust that our manager and company will look after our career and personal interests. The more your company demonstrates that it does look after these interests, the more discretionary effort you unlock. Importantly, the goal for a manager is to achieve both the company's and the individual's goals simultaneously.

The hardest thing for many sales leaders is to maintain a 'true' intent through both good and bad times. In good times, it is easier for companies to deliver on their unwritten commitment to serve the personal and career interests of their employees. The challenge for those looking to motivate performance from sales teams is to link it to the company's growth ambitions, rather than linking it to good and bad times. It is entirely possible that a company is hitting its stock market sales and profit predictions, but the sales team is still considered to be underperforming. This is because today's sales numbers are a result of the business development activity from six months ago. Therefore, people are managed today on the numbers they need to achieve in six months' time. The fear of missing these targets can mean teams spend more time feeling like they are under-performing even when they are performing well. After hitting a personal best three months in a row, I remember saying to my manager 'On my gravestone will be engraved enough was never quite enough.'

In hard times, or times when the pressure is on, it is easy for managers to focus on the result that is needed and forget to communicate how the current plan does or does not deliver on an individual's personal expectations. Through the 2008–2011 recession you could regularly hear employees saying 'the company is doing this' or 'the company could be doing that'. What they were expressing was a feeling that the company was working against their interests, whereas the opposite was often true. The gap in understanding was due to managers not making time to explain how the plan was aimed at helping them keep their jobs and progress their careers. Communication (or a lack of it) is at the heart of this misunderstanding and it is these situations that largely determine how people feel about your approach to performance management.

Managers that want to demonstrate to their employees that they take their interests just as seriously as company interests would do well to consider the following four principles:

Principle 1: Goals not targets

I have a belief that the difference between goals and targets is who owns them. Targets are typically perceived as being owned by a manager, ie you are new in a sales role, your manager will give you a sales target and possibly some target KPIs. Goals, on the other hand, are typically set by an individual. Goals are statements of personal aspiration and engage a higher level of commitment from an individual. This does not mean that targets do not inspire effort: they do. However, if a situation becomes challenging an individual is more likely to work harder for a goal than a target.

It is possible to succeed without goals. However, research shows time and again that individuals with goals tend to be more committed to achieving them.[4] This is why it is so important that managers make the effort to learn what individuals want out of work. While everyone has an interest in earning money, it is what they want to do with that money that a manager needs to know about, be it buying a house, supporting a family or further learning... Achievement of these goals is a large part of what drives sales consultants in your team. The art of a manager is helping individuals set goals within work that help them get what they want either inside or outside of work.

Principle 2: Influence over compulsion

It's one thing to get someone to do something when you are standing next to them. It's quite another to get them working the way you want them to when your back is turned. Successful managers know that the best results come from helping someone want to do a task rather than making them do it. As a leader looking to influence behaviour it may be worth dusting off the Sales 101 books. Importantly, just like a sales process, an 'influencing' approach to leadership is a two-way dialogue focused on reaching mutually beneficial agreement.

Principle 3: Frustrated FOR vs frustrated WITH

I cannot deny that at times I have been very frustrated with individuals who have worked for me. On many occasions I have expressed my frustration with individuals' behaviour. I have also been on the receiving end of my own manager's frustration with my performance While I cannot vouch for what those who worked for me felt, I know from a personal perspective my feelings depended on what I felt the intent behind the frustration was. Sometimes I would have felt that the frustration was WITH me, it gave me the impression their frustration stemmed from them not getting what they wanted (ie hitting a target). At other times my manager's tone and approach indicated they were frustrated FOR me, meaning they were frustrated because now I would not get what I wanted. When someone says 'I am disappointed with you' (often a parent), it has such a big effect on us, because it infers that your own actions have let you down. It's a lot more effective than if someone just rants at you. Next time you are wanting to express your frustration with someone in your team think 'Am I frustrated WITH them or FOR them?' If your answer is WITH, think about how you can temper your tone before you share your views.

Principle 4: Why should I work for you?

A great way to focus your mind and the minds of other managers in your organization is to think about what employees gain from working for you, other than some cash and a place to hang out for a few hours every day. I imagine you spend a significant amount of time crafting a value proposition that specifically meets the needs of your clients. You also invest time and energy proving you deliver against that proposition. But do you build a similar employer or leadership proposition for those in your team or those looking to join your company? If you do, well done, you are in the minority. Can you prove it?

The best response I have had in one of my workshops during the last 12 months was from a manager who described how, on day one of a new person starting, he sits down and has what he calls 'the chat'. In 'the chat' he says 'While you work for me, my job is to ensure that when you leave my team you are able to get a better role than if you had never worked in my team. I will always work to help you get to the next stage of your career. Some days will be progression days, others you will be doing what needs to be done. But over time you will move closer towards your goals.'

Self-assessment: Leadership approach

Ask yourself the following questions to begin to assess whether your leadership approach is sufficiently focused on serving your team members' interests equally to your own.

1 Does my performance management approach focus more on targets or goals?

2 How confident are the members of my team at pushing back when they are asked to do something they disagree with?

3 When I do not get what I want, how do I express my disappointment or frustration with the team or individuals?

4 Do you know why anyone should work for you?

What is your current approach to performance management?

The traditional sales environment is typified in movies such as *Glengarry Glen Ross* and *Boiler Room*. In these movies 'coffee is for closers' (from *Glengarry Glen Ross*) and you do whatever it takes to convert your leads into sales. The approach to performance management is 'If you are not willing or able to do whatever it takes then you can leave.'

In contrast most sales professionals are increasingly involved in longer, more consultative and relationship-driven sales processes. In addition, individuals value autonomy more highly than in the past. This means management teams have had to adapt their approach to performance management. Many companies have found it difficult to adapt their approach. Sales directors and CEOs still need their sales forecasts for this week, month, quarter or beyond.

The challenge for leaders is how to create a sales environment that balances the need for sufficient sales activity to be performed to fill the sales funnel, with giving sales consultants the independence to nurture a longer and more complicated sales process.

Companies typically choose (consciously or unconsciously) one of five ways of managing their performance:

Approach 1: Controlling approach

This is the culture where there is a very clear definition of what needs to be done, when it needs to be done and how it needs to be done. There is typically a high level of expectation, high levels of structure to the day and a focus on input sales activity KPIs. Review meetings take place frequently and focus on the volume of business development activity, the quality of execution and actions being taken to hit sales targets. This approach does not change irrespective of how well a sales consultant performs.

The downsides of this approach are that employees can feel micro managed, which in turn can lead to higher levels of staff turnover across all levels of sales experience. It can also impact customer service levels as sales teams can often care more about hitting a KPI metric than whether the customer is getting the right solution.

There are, however, some good features of a controlling approach to performance management that all sales teams can benefit from.

Figure 12.1 The controlling approach

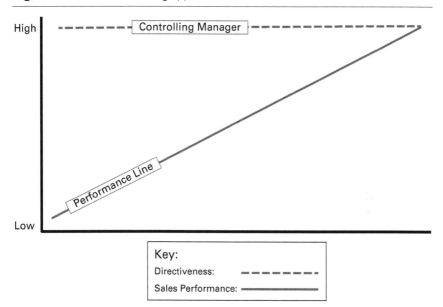

Expectation and accountability

A controlling approach to performance management has an inbuilt expectation that you need to perform and you will be held accountable for your level of performance. When you do reach a target level of performance, expectations rise again. Every level of management keeps expecting more from their teams and typically has a performance review structure that allows daily or weekly feedback between managers and the sales professional. Underlying this is both an implicit and explicit understanding of the consequences of underperformance.

Sales processes

A crystal clear sales process and a step-by-step approach to becoming successful is critical for organizations whose growth depends upon being able to bring in new sales staff and getting them productive quickly. Your sales processes are in effect documentation of what your best people do to succeed and, in turn, the approach you encourage your new sales staff to follow day to day. It is important because a significant amount of business development activity happens over email, social media or on mobile phones. This can make it harder for newer members of the sales team to learn from their peers. I often ask clients 'If I sat in your office for three days, what would I learn about how to be successful in your organization?' The chances are that I would learn about the work ethic and how you treat customers, but would I learn who the target customers are? How to handle objections? What makes a good lead? What makes a good deal?

Key Performance Indicators

So let's talk about the thing that salespeople hate most: KPIs. I am going to put it out there: I believe KPIs are great when an organization is trying to build a positive sales culture. While culture itself is intangible, being able to measure how the business behaves is key to knowing whether a business, team or individual is making progress. Knowing we are making progress is a big motivator.

The reason that KPIs get such a bad press is that they are misused. Too often in controlling environments, the achievement of KPIs becomes disconnected from the role they play in supporting the development of a strong sales pipeline.

The benefits of using KPIs is that they provide structure and understanding for both sales professionals and managers. When someone is new to a sales role, closing a deal can seem pretty abstract. If the goal of the manager is to help the sales professional to achieve consistent self-sustaining performance, then they need to let the sales professional know which activities need to take place when and how much they need to put in to get the desired result. Once they understand this, they can work on improving the effectiveness of what they do to improve results.

Approach 2: Laissez faire approach

This approach to performance management operates on the central principle that 'we treat everyone like grown-ups and they know what to do to hit their target'. KPIs and performance metrics are only infrequently used. One-to-one meetings tend to be informal chats and performance-orientated discussions tend to be focused on improving attitudes rather than must-do actions or activities. Experienced sales professionals can thrive in this environment as they are given the autonomy they want to work the way they choose. The flip side is that the reduced visibility of the pipeline means that sales dips are harder to pre-empt and sales forecasting can be challenging. In this environment it can be challenging to get less experienced members of the sales team as they are a less defined sales process and lower levels of accountability mean speed to sales productivity can be low.

There are, however, some good features of a laissez faire approach to performance management that all sales teams can benefit from.

Independence to decide for yourself what is best

One of the most motivational aspects of the laissez faire approach is that individuals get the freedom to determine what they do to build their sales pipeline and how they do it. The implicit assumption is that the sales professional can be relied upon to do what is needed to hit their sales target.

Figure 12.2 Laissez faire approach

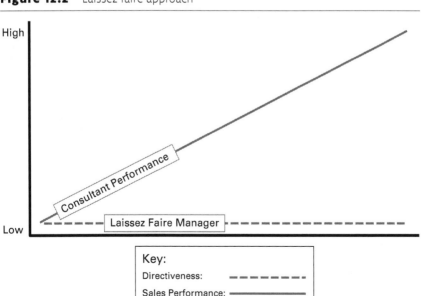

Customer-centricity

Another benefit of the laissez faire culture is that a relaxed environment is more conducive to higher levels of customer service. That is not to say that the controlling environment does not care about customer service, but its importance is sometimes lost in the drive for results and need to hit KPIs.

The main characteristic of a customer-centric sales environment is the willingness to focus on the long-term client relationship over the quick win. The long-term approach seeks to match the business development process with the buyer's purchasing process. Where a client is already using another company's service, the focus is on showing how your company can be a contingency solution if their existing provider fails or they want to widen their supply base.

Laissez faire environments also tend to give clients the time to think before making a decision, versus pushing for an immediate decision. Whereas a sales professional in a controlling environment may chase a client for feedback 20 minutes after sending a proposal, because they need the deal before month end, the laissez faire environment sales professional is more likely to give the client time to make their decision.

Approach 3: The see-saw approach

In this environment, both the laissez faire and the controlling approaches exist. However, they do not exist simultaneously. In good times or when the pipeline is strong, managers take a laissez faire approach. Then when the pipeline starts to look light or sales results are poor, the controlling approach is adopted and everyone, irrespective of performance level, is managed by metrics and a highly structured approach. A catalyst for this change could be poor results or a director getting back from a board meeting or a conference call where they received a 'tune up' from the CEO. The only certainty is that a change in approach is coming. This can be very demotivational for the team as one day they may be being congratulated and the next being told they need to pick up the phone more.

Figure 12.3   The see-saw approach

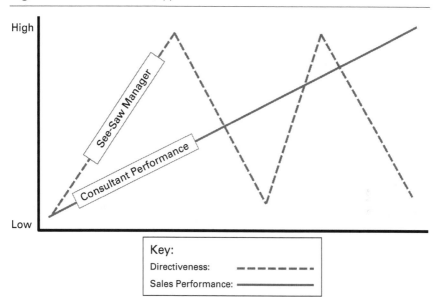

Approach 4: The on/off approach

In this environment, how people are managed at the start of their career is very similar to the controlling culture. They are told what to do and held accountable for doing those things. However, this changes once a certain level of performance has been achieved, and the management style switches to a laissez faire approach to performance. What this often feels like from the perspective of the sales professional is that one day their manager is on every move they make, the next the manager leaves them alone assuming they know all they need to know. When done poorly, it is like a 16-year-old coming home from school to find their parents have moved out, leaving a note saying 'Congratulations, you are ready to live alone: good luck!'

Approach 5: Independence via performance approach

This approach exists informally already within many sales teams. When sales performance is low, there is a high level of direction from the sales manager. As performance improves, an individual is given more independence. What this approach does is formalize what happens informally. This means how much autonomy a salesperson

Figure 12.4   The on/off approach

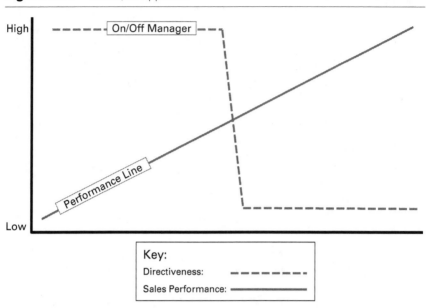

gets is directly linked to sales performance. It works because it takes the best aspects of the controlling and laissez faire approaches to help managers manage each salesperson in their team as an individual. when sales performance is low, managers will push for more sales activity and inspect the quality of sales activity performed. When sales performance is high managers may only want a monthly forecast.

My observations of seeing companies use this approach is that they are able to both retain top performing team members while also being able to make new sales consultants productive quickly.

The reason I feel this explicit approach results in higher levels of motivation is that it relies on established motivational theory, the self-determination theory of motivation initially developed by Edward L Deci and Richard M Ryan,[5] although many readers will be more familiar with it from Dan Pinks' book *Drive: The surprising truth about what motivates us* (2011).[6]

The premise of self-determination theory is that we are intrinsically motivated by three things: Autonomy, Mastery and Purpose. This approach to performance management works in my view because it firstly explicitly states that giving individuals Autonomy is the desired goal of the organization. Secondly it explicitly outlines that Mastery (the better you perform) is intrinsically connected with Autonomy. What I believe this does is inspire higher levels of self-motivation

Figure 12.5   Independence via performance approach

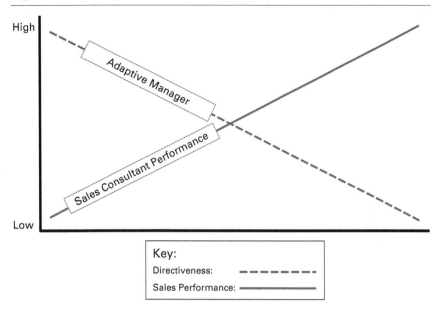

from those that desire autonomy as it clearly sets out the conditions for achieving the autonomy they desire.

Implementing the independence via performance (IVP) approach

The principles we are working towards when implementing the IVP approach are:

1 Everyone is accountable for upholding the values of the organization/team.

2 Structure and direction is provided for less experienced sales consultants or lower-performing individuals.

3 Individuals receive incrementally more independence in how the sales process is executed as sales performance improves.

4 High-performing individuals receive high levels of independence, but business development activities are reviewed on an ad-hoc basis.

5 There are clearly defined and communicated performance management criteria, where the management approach changes depending upon performance.

NOTE Throughout the following I will be referring to Table 12.1.

Table 12.1 IVP – performance management framework

Outline Best Practice	Level 1: Metrics & Measures 3 Mth Av = £0– £7,000pm	Level 2: Metrics & Measures 3 Mth Av = £7,500–£11,000pm	Level 3: Metrics & Measures 3 Mth Av = £11,000–£16,000pm	Level 4: Metrics & Measures 3 Mth Av = £16,000+
Lead Generation & Qualification • Sourcing of leads or prospective clients • Organization of leads or potential clients in CRM • Sharing lead information with other departments (other teams or marketing) • Qualification of leads through conversations with potential clients	• Number of new unqualified leads or potential clients sourced • Number of phone conversations with prospective clients • Number of new 'qualified' leads or potential clients	• Number of new 'qualified' leads or potential clients		
Relationship Nurturing & Lead Conversion • Building credibility with clients through regular contact, business questioning and sharing high-value content • Face-to-face meetings with high potential clients • Managing lead conversion/ pitch process when clients have defined need	• Number of clients in contact cycle • Number of client meetings • Number of qualified pitches • £ of opportunities at pitch stage • Client meeting/pitch ratio • Pitch/Win Ratio	• Number of client meetings • Number of qualified pitches • £ of opportunities at pitch stage • Client meeting/pitch ratio • Pitch/Win Ratio	• Number of qualified pitches • £ of opportunities at pitch stage • Client meeting/pitch ratio • Pitch/Win Ratio	• £ of opportunities at pitch stage • Client meeting/ pitch ratio • Pitch/Win Ratio

Client Satisfaction & Retention (post service delivery) • Understand client's feeling on service delivery and value • Maintain ongoing contact to pitch for future business • Provide value added 'advice' to deepen relationship	• Number of past clients contacted in last 60 days • Client satisfaction score of <insert figure>	• Number of past clients contacted in last 60 days • Client satisfaction score of <insert figure> • % of clients given additional chances at pitching • % of clients retained year on year	• Client satisfaction score of <insert figure> • % of clients given additional chances at pitching • % of clients retained year on year	• Client satisfaction score of <insert figure> • % of clients given additional chances at pitching • % of clients retained year on year
Client Expansion • Maintain account expansion plan for a list of <insert number> high potential accounts • Actively expand line manager network in organization, buyers, influencers and support functions (ie procurement) • Introduce additional Business Lines to relevant line managers		• Number of new line managers found and engaged • Number of face-to-face meetings • Number of new pitch opportunities	• Number of new line managers found and engaged • Number of face-to-face meetings • Number of new pitch opportunities • % share of total client spend • £ growth in revenue YoY	• Number of new line managers found and engaged • Number of face-to-face meetings • Number of new pitch opportunities • % share of total client spend • £ growth in revenue YoY
Review & Planning Meeting Cadence	Weekly & Monthly	Monthly & Quarterly	Monthly or Quarterly	Quarterly or Half Yearly

The following text assumes a sales professional's role begins focused on new business development, progressing to account management and expansion as the client base grows.

Step 1: Sales process and measures

The first step in this process is for an organization to be clear on its sales process and the activities that need to be performed on a daily, weekly and monthly basis. Once you have this you can then start to add meaningful metrics that either outline the quantity of what has been done or the quality with which the process is being executed.

If you already have a 'controlling' approach to managing the sales pipeline, you will already have this map. This mapping process does not have to be a complicated process and can be completed on one sheet of paper. All you need to do is divide the paper into sections where each one represents a stage of the sales process.

For a typical sales process the sections could be as follows:

- lead generation and qualification;
- relationship nurturing and lead conversion;
- client satisfaction and retention;
- client expansion.

Under each stage of the sales process, define what an individual should be expected to be doing at each stage of the process. If appropriate, you could add who is responsible if multiple people are involved in the process. Lastly, you should outline the key metrics that measure business development activity input and effectiveness ratios that would measure how well the activities are being performed.

Example

Lead generation and qualification

Key activities

- sourcing of leads or prospective clients:
  - ie contacting past clients;

- – ie networking (social media or physical events);
- – ie referrals and recommendations from existing network;
- organization of leads or prospective clients in CRM;
- sharing lead information with other departments (other teams or marketing);
- qualification of leads through conversations with potential clients.

Key metrics and ratios

- number of new unqualified leads or potential clients sourced;
- number of phone conversations with prospective clients;
- number of new 'qualified' leads or potential clients.

Step 2: Define performance management bandings

In this step the leadership team should define the number of performance levels and what levels of sales or fees would be associated with each level. You can see from the example in Table 12.1 that the company uses four different levels and calculates performance on a three-month average. You will have your own way of measuring sales performance; the key is that each of the bandings you choose represents a sufficient level of performance to allow you to feel the individual is self-sufficient in the areas you are soon to relax your focus on.

Step 3: Define measures, metrics and behaviours

For each banding, the leadership team should create a benchmark pipeline that will provide guidance on which part of the sales pipeline managers will be paying most attention to. You can see from the example in Table 12.1 that, as performance improves, managers leave behind certain metrics and pick up new metrics that they feel are important at this stage of performance.

Step 4: Review focus and cadence

Now that you have your performance management blueprint, you can define what your performance meeting cycle will be. While the frequency may be different according to the level of performance, everyone should have a regular one-to-one meeting with their manager. You can see from Table 12.1 that meeting frequency changes from weekly to half-yearly as performance levels improve.

Naturally, it is easier to write these four stages than to create and implement them in your own business. However, the goal of this four-step exercise is to give you a guide as to how you can structure a graduated approach to providing sales consultants with additional independence as performance improves.

Whichever of the above approaches you have in your organization it has its pros and cons. I imagine each reader will have their own preference. However, there is one thing that is even more important than the approach an organization takes to performance management and it's this: that the organization is open to its staff and potential staff about the approach it takes. Tell employees how their performance management will work and stick to it. Motivation and discretionary effort can be disproportionately affected when an organization says it is one thing, then acts in the opposite way. Imagine you join an organization that says 'We treat you like an adult' and then your manager reviews every call you make every day. Or you work for an organization that says it delivers great training and provides you with a structure to progress, then you are left to get on with it...

As always, there is no right or wrong approach. It is just that you need to be consistent in what you say and how you act. That is of paramount importance.

Once you are clear on what you are, you can craft your pitch and then run your organization according to those principles. The best example of a company being clear about its approach to performance management is Netflix. If you go to Google and type 'Netflix culture slideshare'[7] you will find a super presentation from the Netflix founder. In the presentation, they lay out their values, hiring philosophy and performance management approach. I encourage you to go to slide 38, titled 'Our high performance culture is not right for everyone' and see what they say about their performance management culture.

What is always interesting is that when I run workshops on performance management approach, it always surprises me how evangelical managers are about their performance management cultures. Managers in controlling companies struggle with the thought of not having clarity of how the sales pipeline is moving day to day and trusting whether staff will be working hard when their backs are turned. Many managers from laissez faire environments often have spent portions of their careers in highly controlling environments and have such negative feelings towards KPIs and structure from their previous experiences that they want nothing to do with traditional approaches to managing the sales pipeline.

How to run motivational review meetings

It is not possible to talk about performance management without discussing the performance review meeting.

If I told you that you were about to have a review meeting with your manager, how would you feel? If one of your team were told they were about to have a one-to-one review meeting with you, how would they feel?

Responses to these meeting requests tell you a lot about your organization's ability to unlock discretionary effort in your teams. Because a reluctance to have a one-to-one with your manager may indicate either a lack of buy-in to the manager and in turn a desire to 'go the extra mile' (although there may be other reasons as well).

I imagine during your career you have worked for a manager where you generally left review meetings feeling worse than you went in. I am equally sure you have had managers where after meetings you felt energized and motivated to perform. So, on this basis you know what a good meeting should feel like. How would you rate your one-to-one review meetings? Do they motivate the individuals that participate in them with you? Have you asked for feedback?

While no manager intentionally sets out to run meetings that are demotivational, the chances are that someone in your team finds one-to-one meetings with you demotivational. Should you care? It is probably the awkward naysayer anyway... The reality is that if you want to unlock the discretionary effort of the team as a whole, running motivational meetings for everyone (even the naysayers) is key.

Research carried out by the research and advisory firm, Bersin by Deloitte, in 2014 (*Human Capital Trends Report*, 2014[8]) highlighted that only 6 per cent of the 583 respondents felt that their performance management process drove engagement and high performance. The challenge for many companies is that it is increasingly difficult to apply a score to someone's performance when much of their work is knowledge, relationship-based and dependent on collaboration.

Laszlo Bock in his book *Work Rules*[9] described how Google tried to change their 'score' score-based approach (they have a 41-point scale, from 1.0 (awful) to 5.0 (astounding)). The approach they ended up with using was a rating system that started at the low end with 'needs improvement', through 'consistently meets expectations', 'exceeds expectations', 'strongly exceeds expectations' and lastly 'superb'. What I like about Google's approach is that it moves away from a forced scoring system towards an approach that focuses on someone's 'perceived ability' to deliver against expectations. In turn, rather than haggling over a 0.1 or 0.2 rating, managers are encouraged to have more open discussions about why someone is in a particular category.

However, for sales teams and individuals with revenue targets, performance management is a clearer cut process. Sales meetings tend to be more frequent, something that Bersin by Deloitte's research highlights as a positive. However, such meetings often are heavily focused on sales forecasts and sales activities for the previous period. While useful to the manager, this does not necessarily allow for managers to help the sales professional with their individual needs. This can mean someone leaves a one-to-one review meeting without having received any proactive support in helping them achieve their goals in the coming month/quarter. This is not an outcome that inspires higher levels of motivation.

When thinking about how to improve your performance management process, the best place to start is not theory X or theory Y. Instead, focus on how you and those in your team feel about your current process. The process of research does not need to be any more than you and your team asking each other a series of questions.

Review meeting assessment

Manager questions:

- What do I want from performance review meetings?
- What do I not currently get from the meetings?

Sales consultant questions:

- What do I want from my review meetings?
- What do I not currently get from my review meetings?

If your team answers these questions it may be that you find similarities between what you and your team wants from the process. More importantly you will discover if there is a disconnect between what you both want and what you both get.

Below I have listed a few areas where there may be a disconnect between how you approach the meetings and whether or not they are considered motivational by individuals in your team.

1: Refocus the intent

One of the common frustrations with review meetings is that they only serve the agenda of the manager, rather than the individual's agenda. There is a paradox here in that usually, a company can only hit its target if the individuals in the team hit theirs. A phrase I have already used in the book is worth repeating at this point: it's 'frustrated FOR, not frustrated WITH'. It is so important that managers keep this phrase at the front of their minds in order to realign the focus of their intent away from themselves and the company and towards the individual.

Try rephrasing some of your inner thoughts to keep you focused on what your sales consultants want rather than what you want.

2: Focus on the future

A second area of improvement is switching the focus of the meeting from the past to the future. Here's the scenario: the manager walks into the room thinking 'How am I going to cover poor sales activity again?' Meanwhile, the consultant walks in thinking 'I did not do enough activity last month. What excuses can I give? As long as I promise to do more next month I should be OK.' And so the cycle continues. By focusing the meeting on the future instead, both parties can arrive thinking about what the plan needs to be in the coming weeks. Now the meeting can starts with 'Last month was <great, OK or poor>. What are we going to change in order to do better this month?' I know many companies that have dropped the term 'review meetings', calling them 'planning meetings' instead, so as to emphasize the focus on the future.

3: Change ownership of the meeting

When a manager passes the responsibility of preparing for the meeting, the role of the manager changes. It changes from being a reviewer to an advisor. Their role is to check the performance plan and offer coaching to help the individual execute their plan. Yet, so often, there is insufficient or no aligning of individual goals to their organization's strategic goals. A report by Harvard Business Review called *How Employee Alignment Boosts The Bottom Line*[10] found that 70 per cent of respondents said alignment was the greatest hurdle to achieving company strategy. Furthermore, the research found that when companies have aligned, high-performing employees are 2.2 times more likely to be top performers compared with their competition.

4: Coaching not criticism

In the previous section, we discussed the importance of developing both confidence and capability to improve levels of motivation. While many believe training happens in the training room, the reality is that weekly, monthly and quarterly one-to-one meetings between a manager and individuals in their team deliver learning in a very different way. Training courses may well deliver lots of ideas, but it is the two-way dialogue in meetings that helps turn ideas into execution. Therefore, the more meetings focus on successful implementation of ideas or increasing effectiveness of sales activities, the more motivational they will become.

A great productivity tip for review meetings is to make sure in every meeting you have access to a PC where the CRM can be accessed. This will help managers have more objective conversations, discussing specific activities that have occurred in the past or are occurring in the future (note: it also increases the likelihood of the CRM being viewed as a sales-enabling tool).

5: Regular cadence

The book *The 4 Disciplines of Execution* by McCheesney, Covey and Huling[11] highlighted the importance of a regular cadence being key to implementing lasting change. We have all been part of 'initiatives' that everyone focuses on for a few weeks only to be dropped once people stop talking about it. Regular review meetings allow managers to continually focus on key areas of change until they become embedded in day-to-day activities. The frequency of your one-to-one meeting process may depend on the speed of your sales process or the capability of the individual.

The FAST review meeting

A simple way to get started on engaging both managers and employees in the performance review process is to have an **agreed** structure of what a meeting will entail and what each person is responsible for in terms of preparing for the meeting. There is almost an unlimited variation of review forms. However, as a guide I have listed a simple meeting template that has been successfully adopted by my clients for weekly tactically-focused sales one-to-one meetings.

The FAST meeting template is intended as a structure for meetings that occur regularly, are relatively unstructured and require little preparation from either party. The purpose of the meeting is to help the manager understand how well the sales professional is organizing and conducting their business development activity.

Here's what the acronym stands for:

F: Feeling: The first stage of any performance meeting needs to focus on how the person is feeling. While the manager may have a set agenda, they will make little progress if the person they want to influence is not in the right frame of mind for change. It may be the person is feeling fine and so the manager can move on. However, if the person is stressed, unhappy or upset, these feelings need to be addressed before progress with the remainder of the meeting can be made. Once managers take this approach, they become more proactive in discussing feelings and emotional challenges.

A: Activity: Importantly, the discussion regarding activity focuses not on volume, but on effectiveness of past activity. With a forward-looking approach, the manager gains more detail about how client meetings can be followed up and converted into opportunities and what the next steps are to convert a small client into a key client.

S: Sales: This is the manager's opportunity to discuss their team member's sales pipeline. Historically, meetings chewed up time looking at deals that closed and reviewing deals that did not occur. In the forward-looking approach, managers focus on current opportunities and look to help with coaching and advice to maximize the chances of successfully converting any opportunities. Past situations are only discussed in the context of 'lessons to be learnt' and to be applied to current situations to mitigate and manage risks.

T: Targets: Whether you prefer the word 'targets' or 'goals', the end of every meeting needs to result in a set of measurable commitments that both the manager and team member can reference back to in the coming days and weeks. Almost every reader will be familiar with the SMART approach to target- and goal-setting, as first mentioned in the November 1981 issue of Management Review.[12] SMART stands for: specific, measurable, agreed upon, realistic and time-bound. Many managers make the mistake of over-focusing on the SMT bits of SMART: specific, measurable and time-bound. The keys to successful implementation are **agreed upon** and **realistic**.

In summary, this approach focuses on the manager and sales professional having an open dialogue about the things that are most important to each other's success, rather than focusing on a formal and rigid process.

Summary

This has been a monster chapter, mainly because a company's approach to performance plays such an important role in motivating individuals in organizations. I hope that there are a few key things that you will take away. Firstly, that your own attitude to what performance management means is key to your success. Are you there to make people do their jobs or to help them get what they want out of work? Secondly, autonomy and mastery are key intrinsic motivators to every person that works for you. So the more you can build the achievement of autonomy and mastery into your performance management approach the greater the levels of intrinsic motivation you can achieve. Lastly, please remember that one-to-one review meetings are there to motivate individuals to higher levels of performance. So the more ownership you can give for planning the meetings and the more you can focus on the future, the more motivational they will be.

References

1 Gallup (2017) *State of the American Workplace Report* http://www.gallup.com/reports/199961/state-american-workplace-report-2017.aspx [last accessed 14/4/18]

2 Schwantes, M (2017) *Why Do People Quit Their Jobs, Exactly? Here's the Entire Reason, Summed Up in 1 Sentence*, https://www.inc.com/amp/147786.html [last accessed 14/4/18]

3 There are various forms of this quote attributed to a number of people such as Mike Tyson and John F Milburn

4 Locke, E A and Latham, G P (1990) *A Theory of Goal Setting and Task Performance*, Prentice Hall, Upper Saddle River, NJ

5 Wikipedia, Self Determination Theory https://en.wikipedia.org/wiki/Self-determination_theory [last accessed 14/4/18]

6 Pink, D (2011) *Drive: The surprising truth about what motivates us*, Canongate Books

7 Gill, B (2016) *Netflix Culture Deck* https://www.slideshare.net/BarbaraGill3/netflix-culture-deck [last accessed 14/4/18]

8 Garr, S and Laikopoulos, A (2014) *Performance Management Is Broken: Replacing 'rank and yank' with coaching and development*, Deloitte Insights https://dupress.deloitte.com/dup-us-en/focus/human-capital-trends/2014/hc-trends-2014-performance-management.html#endnote-sup-1 [last accessed 14/4/18]

9 Bock, L (2016) *Work Rules*, John Murray Publishers

10 Harvard Business Review, *How Employee Alignment Boosts The Bottom Line*, Harvard Business Publishing https://hbr.org/resources/pdfs/comm/betterworks/19764_HBR_Reports_BetterWorks_May2016.pdf [last accessed 14/4/18]

11 McCheesney, C, Covey, S and Huling, J (2012) *The 4 Disciplines of Execution*, Simon & Schuster

12 Doran, G T (1981) *There's a SMART way to write management's goals and objectives*, Management Review, AMA FORUM, 70 (11): 35–36

Conclusion
A quick recap

When setting out to write this book I set myself a challenge. There are countless books that focus on just one piece of the cultural change or sales growth jigsaw. I wanted to attempt to bring together multiple pieces of this jigsaw to help leaders have a greater awareness of how the pieces may come together to achieve cultural change and sales growth. At times I have wondered why I chose this approach! There are so many jigsaw pieces to changing and improving culture; deciding which ones to include, which to leave out, which to go deep on, which to touch on has been a mammoth task.

So have I succeeded? Only you can judge...

However, let's quickly recap. The central premise of this book is that market changes brought about by digitization, automation and changing buyer behaviour mean that companies are having to work harder than ever to retain and acquire customers. The key challenge this brings is the need for companies to change how they approach their sales process. This means sales teams will need to change their approach. However, it also means more and more individuals in organizations are being drawn in to support the sales process. You only need to talk to a few service engineers, customer success managers, management consultants, accountants, lawyers and many more who are now expected to be part of the sales process, a role completely new to them.

While some companies may choose to do nothing, most will have a plan to either change the nature of the products or solutions they sell, and/or be changing how they approach the sales process. Whichever route a company chooses, success will depend upon inspiring, motivating or cajoling existing employees to change their behaviours. This is where the heart of the challenge lies, because while processes or systems can be changed fairly simply, changing attitudes and behaviours is much harder work.

To facilitate this change my view is that there are three pillars that leaders need to address; building a customer focus in your team; aligning company goals with those of the individuals in the company, and lastly building an environment that supports both individuals and the company to achieve their goals.

Customer focus is vital because the speed of market change means that companies need to be continually refocusing their products and services to what customers want today rather than what they wanted last year. Companies that do not align with customer needs are likely to be left behind. In addition, as more millennials enter the workplace, their reduced emphasis of financial reward as a motivator means companies need to seek other ways to engage their sales and non-sales teams in going the extra mile. Genuinely serving a customer need is a key way to unlock discretionary effort.

Employees are increasingly looking for a more mutually beneficial relationship with the companies they work for. The more companies and managers can align their own goals with the goals of their employees the more likely they are to unlock discretionary effort. Furthermore, employees are less accepting of being a passive passenger on a company's journey. They are wanting their voices and opinions to be heard as the company navigates its way through market challenges. The two behaviours employers and managers need to adopt are taking time to consciously align company objectives with individual goals and then avoiding the 'smart dumb' paradox by actively seeking the views, opinions and ideas from all levels within their teams.

Finally, creating a collaborative approach to business development is critical. The sales process is increasingly too complicated for one person to manage and collaboration is the only way to really find, win and retain customers in today's market. Of all the challenges highlighted in the book, collaboration is one of the most difficult to overcome. Sales has traditionally been the place where individualism thrives and is rewarded. However, when sales processes cross multiple functions, individualism needs to be balanced with the needs of the wider team. Indeed as more individuals become involved in business development activities, unlocking discretionary effort will depend on everyone believing in the capability and intent of the individuals they work with. Sadly, lone wolf sales professionals do not always inspire high levels of effort from those they partner with.

So how is change achieved? By open dialogue. Throughout the book there are exercises and discussions which I hope help you feel more confident in engaging and discussing openly how the company's approach to business development can change to serve the interests of your customers, your employees and also the company itself.

I hope that after reading this book you have insights that you want to share. Whether those insights be good, bad or ugly feel free to reach out to me on either LinkedIn or on www.alexmoyle.co.uk and share your views.

Thanks for reading.
Alex

INDEX